Eric
Twiname

The Rules
Book

Adlard Coles
William Collins Sons & Co. Ltd
8 Grafton Street, London W1X 3LA

First published by Adlard Coles 1977
Reprinted 1977
Reprinted with amendments 1977
Reprinted 1978, 1979
Second edition 1981
Reprinted 1984
Third edition 1985
Reprinted 1985
Fourth edition 1989

British Library Cataloguing in Publication Data
Twiname, Eric
The rules book : the 1989–92 international yacht
racing rules explained.—4th ed.
1. International Yacht Racing Union. Yacht racing
rules   2. Yacht racing—Rules
I. Title   II. Willis, Bryan
797.1′4   GV 826.7

ISBN 0-229-11839-9

Printed in Great Britain by
William Collins Sons Ltd, Glasgow

*Dedication: To my mother and father who
taught me the first rules I knew.*

CONTENTS

ACKNOWLEDGEMENTS

Some of the interpretations and the idea of using an almost comic-strip presentation first appeared in my articles for *Yachts and Yachting* whose readers very usefully pounced on my interpretative mistakes. The International Yacht Racing Union kindly allowed us to reprint sections of the racing rules, and the Royal Yachting Association gave me a unique opportunity to sharpen up my wits and rule knowledge by asking me to join their racing rules committee three years ago.

The manuscript came in for a hard time under the perceptive eyes of Bryan Willis, Andrew Pool, Graham Donald, Nick Martin and the National Sailing coach, Bob Bond, who checked the book for its use in teaching and for ease of understanding. The chairman of the IYRU and RYA racing rules committees, Gerald Sambrooke-Sturgess, was kind enough to read and correct the manuscript as carefully as if he had written it himself. Almost all their suggestions and corrections have been worked into the book.

Clive Gordon and the Parkway Design Group produced the quite superb design and layout with more than just professional competence and imagination. They were also amazingly patient.

Everyone I have dealt with in Adlard Coles and Granada, especially Jeremy Howard-Williams, Bruce Thomas and Rab MacWilliam, have responded with exceptional warmth and enthusiasm to the project. But my biggest debt is to Oliver Freeman. It was Oliver, when managing editor, who persuaded me to write the book and shaped it with me at every step of the way, even when he no longer worked for the company. Did I say my biggest debt? I was forgetting Jill.

To all of you who have helped, thank you.

Eric Twiname
March 1977

Eric's tragic death in 1980 meant a great loss both to his friends and to yachtsmen everywhere. His *Rules Book* has helped countless helmsmen to grasp the principles of the racing rules, and in making the changes necessary for the book to comply with the current rules, I have been careful not to change Eric's unique method of presentation.

Bryan Willis
January 1989

LEARNING THE
RULES

Learning the Rules

The rules of sailing are complex. There's no getting away from that. But there are ways of making rule knowledge much more accessible and the rules themselves easier to understand. This book is written very much with those two aims in mind.

Anyone who races sailing boats needs to know something about the rules. To begin with you only need know enough to get a boat round the course without fouling the others. Later the rules become tactically important because they define what moves you are allowed to make when trying to overtake other boats and, just as important, what tricks other people might legitimately use in trying to overtake you.

So the crucial point about learning the sailing rules is that your knowledge needs to be a working knowledge. There is little point in learning the rules merely to be able to quote chapter and verse. That won't help you on the water, whereas a good working knowledge certainly will, since rule knowledge is a vital department of your racing skills – as important as knowledge of wind and weather.

The International Yacht Racing Union's (IYRU) racing rule book is something most people approach at best reluctantly. For one thing it's usually only approached at all when you've got a problem. Which puts it immediately into the category of garages, police stations and dentists. But with the difference that most times you turn to the rule book you will find something that either you can't quite understand or that contradicts something you thought you did know.

This book therefore approaches the whole problem the other way round, starting from the real live situations that you're liable to come across while racing. So rather than looking for a rule which might apply to the situation in question, you can turn straight to that situation and read which rule applies, how it applies and why it applies. To make this possible, the situations are arranged here, not to the basic logic of the IYRU rule book, but to a logic based on your perception of situations as you meet them on the water.

There are several things that anyone who knows anything at all about sailing will be able to tell you about a collision or near miss, whether they have ever seen a rule book or not. The first thing they'll be able to say is whereabouts on the course the incident happened. They shouldn't find it too difficult either, to say which tacks the boats were on or whether they were tacking or gybing. And already, by answering these questions correctly, over 90 per cent of racing incidents can be eliminated and we are left with, at most, 10 per cent. The sections of the book have therefore been arranged to correspond to parts of the course, with subdivisions into incidents where boats are on opposite tacks, on the same tack, tacking or gybing.

In this way, when you are trying to unravel the rights and wrongs of a particular incident, you can quickly home in on the relevant 5 or 10 per cent of possible incidents. Among these, the one you want will be easy to find. Having found it, you can read why one boat is in the right and the other in the wrong, why a particular rule applies, which rule that is and, on difficult points, which appeals cases support the interpretation. The rule referred to can then be looked up in the IYRU rule book (reproduced in the back of this book, starting on page 93).

So far I have only mentioned the book's use in providing a post-mortem analysis after a rule infringement. But if you're a racing helmsman you constantly need to know just what you can do during a race without infringing any rules. You can certainly build up this knowledge by tearing around the course hitting other boats and being protested against afterwards, but by far the best way to learn is to keep your rule knowledge running in advance of your sailing skills.

Some right-of-way problems are much more common than others, so the situations dealt with here are graded so that you can, if you like, sit down and work up your rule knowledge to a level that fits in with your other racing abilities.

The incidents and situations interpreted in the book are graded on three levels. These levels are:

1. rules everyone who races should know (dealt with on pages 5 to 9)
▌ 2. racing at the top end of a club fleet
▌▌ 3. top-level national and international competition and team racing

For the purpose of learning the rules, the book should not be read from cover to cover in the usual way. That would be too big a bite at once and probably pretty confusing, unless you already know the rules quite well. Instead, the best approach is to decide what level of rule knowledge you want from the book beforehand, then to ignore everything listed as being beyond the level you've set yourself.

Take the example of a helmsman who has raced for a couple of seasons, and who wants to improve his rule knowledge so that he is at least on a par with the people who are winning his club races. His approach to learning would be to read all items marked by one boat (but not those marked by two boats), checking back to any rules referred to, but ignoring the appeal case references.

If you work in this way you needn't read from the front of the book to the back, but will learn faster by picking a particular section – mark-rounding from an offwind leg, for example, – and first studying only that section, rather than trying to take in too much at once. Re-reading, dipping into the book at random – but not yet reading beyond the level you've set yourself – are all useful parts of the learning process. For really keen groups of people, and particularly for children, quizzes are an obvious way of livening up the process.

Learning is also speeded up considerably by using the book as a reference after racing to check the rights and wrongs of any incidents or near misses you experienced during the race. When using the book in this way, of course, you would not restrict yourself to the grading levels, since an incident you want to know about might be one of those rare ones in group 3.

One important word of warning, though. What may look like two identical situations in different sections of the book will sometimes have opposite interpretations. This is because the position on the course is crucial. For example, when two boats collide within two lengths of a mark, the boat in the wrong is liable to be the one that is in the right if you take the mark away and have them in open water on a leg of the course. It is vital to make sure you read and bear in mind the leg of course the boats are on–which is why that information is printed at the top of every page.

The interpretations are, as far as possible, not my own but those of the IYRU, the RYA (Royal Yachting Association) and the USYRU (United States Yacht Racing Union). Throughout I have included references to their most useful published appeals, so anyone can look these up if they want to. At protest meetings – whether you are on the committee or one of the warring parties – the relevant appeal case placed on the table is usually decisive – and gratifying. You are instantly a rule expert. No longer is it a question of 'my opinion is this . . .' but 'this is what the definitive IYRU, RYA or USYRU appeal says', which is difficult for a protest committee to refute, or for a competitor who has just been disqualified to argue about.

The IYRU appeal cases are accepted as definitive anywhere (except in the very rare case of a more recent published national appeal conflicting; then the national appeal might apply in that country). The RYA appeals apply in British clubs and classes and any others under the RYA's jurisdiction; the USYRU appeals apply only in the USA. Elsewhere national appeals of the country concerned govern, but in the absence of a national or IYRU appeal on a point of interpretation for races held outside Britain or the USA, an RYA or USYRU appeal which clarified the point would usually be accepted by a protest committee in that country. The national authority would always have the chance of reversing the decision on appeal – if the dispute went that far.

The rules themselves are revised once every four years and those used in this edition are valid until early 1993. These rules together with the RYA prescriptions can be bought in a booklet from the Royal Yachting Association, Romsey Road, Eastleigh, Hampshire SO5 4YA, England. So can the RYA appeals cases. The IYRU racing rules alone and its appeals can be bought from the IYRU at 60 Knightsbridge, London SW1X 7JX, and USYRU appeals from the USYRU, P.O. Box 229, Newport, Rhode Island, 0284, USA.

THE RULES
EVERYONE WHO
RACES
SHOULD KNOW

An understanding of these first
few pages of introduction to the
rules enables a racing helmsman
to keep out of trouble and
provides the logical framework
which underlies all the right of
way rules, however complex.
These are the most important
four pages in the book.

The sailing rules are designed to prevent collisions and to promote fair sailing. So when boats collide, or when a right-of-way boat is forced to steer clear, the boat in the wrong should be penalised. The voluntary penalty is retirement from the race or, when 720 degree penalties are in force, two full penalty turns. If a helmsman in the wrong does not take the voluntary penalty soon after the incident, another competitor or the race organisers may lodge a protest. In the protest meeting the boat in the wrong is disqualified. The basic right-of-way code is quite simple, but it is important to know that the right-of-way in open water is fundamentally different from that at marks of the course or other obstructions.

Basic right-of-way in open water

When neither boat is about to sail round a mark but are both in open water:

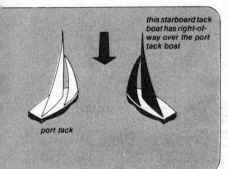

1. A boat on port tack keeps clear of a boat on starboard tack (rule 36).

2. A windward boat keeps clear of a leeward boat (rule 37.1).

3. A boat which is tacking or gybing keeps clear of one that isn't (rule 41).

4. A boat clear astern of another keeps clear of the one ahead when they are both on the same tack (rule 37.2).

Basic right-of-way at a windward mark

At a windward mark – that is a mark of the course which you have been tacking to reach – the basics are:

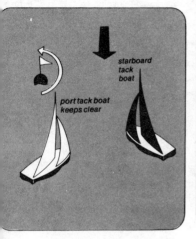

1. When on opposite tacks, take the mark away and apply the principles as in open water (rule 42(a) and 36).

2. When on the same tack, the boat next to the mark must be given room to round by the boat outside (rule 42.1 (a)).

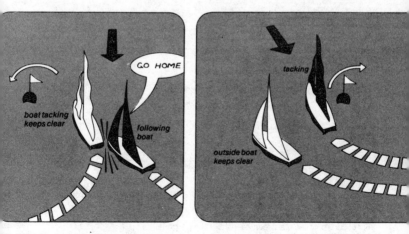

3. When a boat is tacking round the mark, she must keep clear of any following boat (rule 42.2(c)) but any boat outside her must give her room (rule 42.1(a)).

Basic right-of-way at an offwind mark

At an offwind mark – that is one you have sailed to on a close reach, broad reach or run – the basics are:

1. The boat on the inside at the mark must be given room to round (rule 42.1(a)). The port and starboard rule (36) does not apply here.

2. A boat which approaches the mark clear ahead of another has the right to gybe round the mark; the other boat must keep clear (rule 42.2(a)).

3. The boat on the inside must not round so wide that she sails into a boat that is giving her room (rules 36, 37, 41.1).

Basic rights before and at the start

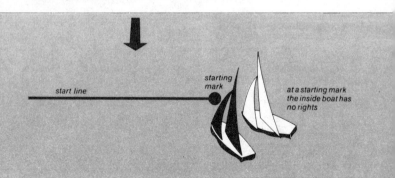

The rules before the start are slightly different in some details from those after the start. Collisions are common before the start, and it is important to realise that if you are either out of control or are pre-occupied in adjusting a halyard, you can be penalised in a collision with a boat which has right-of-way. So if you're going to mess about with your boat just before the start, make sure you're on starboard tack. If you infringe a rule in the 'preparatory period' (usually five minutes before the start), you will have to retire or take a penalty.

At a starting mark an inside windward overlapping boat has no right to claim room when approaching the line to start (rule 42.4).

The luffing rule

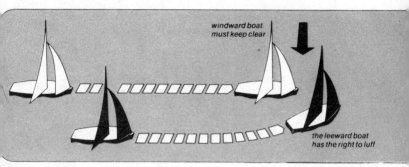

windward boat
must keep clear

the leeward boat
has the right to luff

There is another rule which is worth knowing about right from the beginning: this is the luffing rule (rule 38). When you're overtaking another boat to windward the leeward helmsman has the right to protect his wind by throwing his boat head to wind as sharply as he likes. If he hits you, you are the one who'll be penalised for the collision. A luff may only be done slowly before the start (rule 40).

Boats, cruising, in other races and motor boats

The IYRU yacht racing rules apply only between boats which are racing, either in the same or different races. Sailing boats have right-of-way over motor boats, but in confined waters ships have right-of-way over yachts. It should always be remembered that the rules are primarily intended to enable people to avoid collisions.

When a boat which is racing meets one which is cruising, or when sailing between sunset and sunrise, a different set of right-of-way rules apply: they are the International Regulations for Preventing Collisions at Sea (IRPCS). Although essentially the same as the basic IYRU rules explained above, there are two important differences! The IRPCS code does not allow luffing, and a boat which is overtaking must keep clear, regardless of which tacks the boats concerned are on. As a matter of courtesy, though, boats not racing should always do their best to keep clear of those racing.

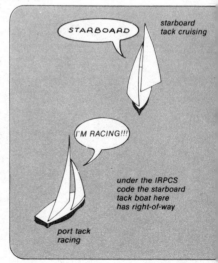

STARBOARD

starboard
tack cruising

I'M RACING!!!

under the IRPCS
code the starboard
tack boat here
has right-of-way

port tack
racing

9

DEFINITIONS

The rules are built on simple and precise ideas; these are the building blocks and they must be understood if the full meaning of the rules is to become clear.

◀ Racing

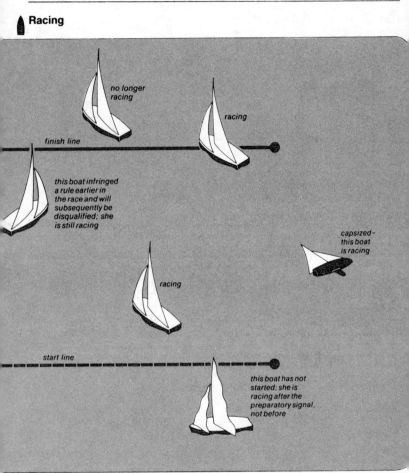

The international racing rules apply to boats which are racing or about to race. Penalties for infringing the rules come into force after the preparatory signal (usually 5 minutes before the starting signal) and apply to a boat until she has finished and cleared the finish line. A boat may then only be penalised under the rules for seriously hindering a boat which is still racing. (Definition, Part I, rule 31.2).

A boat which infringes a rule without realising it and which therefore continues racing and is later disqualified after a protest does not lose her right-of-way status during the race. She is racing throughout and carries exactly the same rights under the rules as other boats racing (IYRU appeal case 2). To continue to race knowing that a rule has been infringed is a violation of fundamental rule D (Accepting Penalties).

Port tack and starboard tack

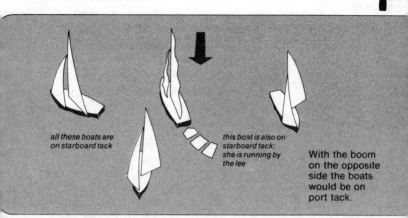

all these boats are
on starboard tack

this boat is also on
starboard tack;
she is running by
the lee

With the boom
on the opposite
side the boats
would be on
port tack.

A boat is on starboard tack when her mainsail is on her port side. Conversely, a boat is on port tack when her mainsail is on her starboard side. Helmsmen who have problems knowing which tack they are on can usefully paint 'starboard tack' on the starboard side of the boom and 'port tack' on the port side. It saves having to think.

Close-hauled and free

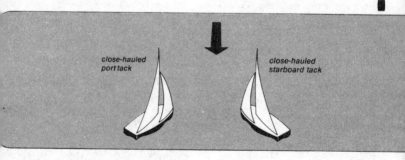

close-hauled
port tack

close-hauled
starboard tack

The term 'close-hauled' defines a direction of sailing in relation to the wind; this is different for different classes of boat and to a lesser degree among boats of the same class. The official rule book definition reads: 'A yacht is close-hauled when sailing by the wind as close as she can lie with advantage in working to windward'.

The terms 'beating', 'beating to windward' and 'on the wind' are all sometimes used to mean close-hauled.

Windward and leeward

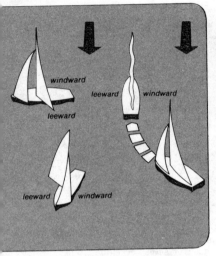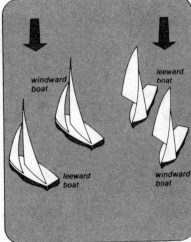

The leeward side of a boat is the side that the mainsail is being carried; or if head to wind, on the side the mainsail was before she became head to wind. The opposite side is the windward side.

When two boats are overlapped on the same tack the leeward one is the one on the other's leeward side. The other boat is the windward one.

Luffing

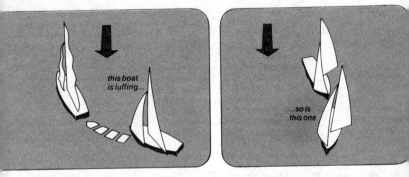

A boat which is luffing is altering course towards the wind. Other phrases commonly used (though not in the rules) to mean the same as luffing are: 'hardening up', 'pointing up' and 'putting the helm down'.

Bearing away

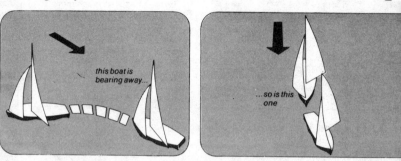

A boat which is bearing away is altering course away from the wind. Bearing away stops when the boat begins to gybe. Other phrases commonly used (though not in the rules) to mean the same as bearing away are: 'bearing off', 'bearing down', 'freeing off' and 'putting the helm up'.

Tacking

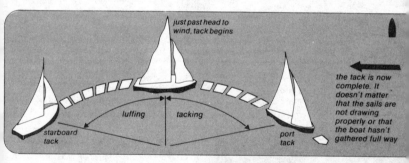

When people talk about tacking they usually mean the whole manoeuvre from first putting the helm down to getting under way on the new tack. The rule book definition is much narrower than this. The boat first luffs, and her tack is not defined as beginning until after she has passed through the eye of the wind. Tacking continues until the boat has reached a close-hauled course on the new tack.

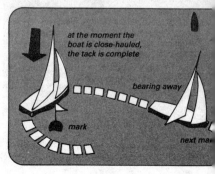

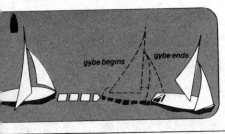

Gybing

Gybing happens much more quickly than tacking. The gybe begins when, with the wind aft, the boom crosses the centreline; it ends when the mainsail has filled on the other tack.

Overlapped, clear astern and clear ahead

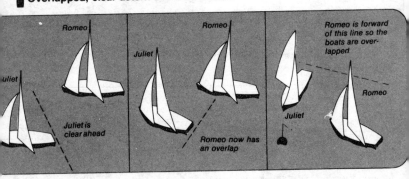

'A yacht is clear astern of another when her hull and equipment in normal position are abaft an imaginary line projected abeam from the aftermost point of the other's hull and equipment in normal position. The other yacht is clear ahead...' (Definition in Part I of the rule book.)

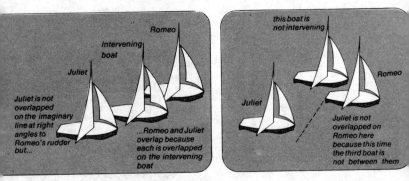

'The yachts overlap if neither is clear astern; or if, although one is clear astern, an intervening yacht overlaps both of them...' (Definition.)

Obstruction

'An obstruction is any object, including a vessel under way, large enough to require a yacht, if more than one overall length away from it, to make a substantial alteration of course to pass on one side or the other, or any object which can be passed on one side only, including a buoy when the yacht in question cannot safely pass between it and the shoal or object which it marks.' (Definition).

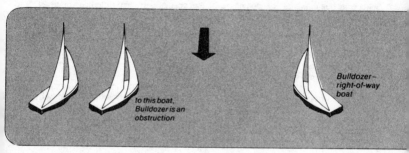

to this boat, Bulldozer is an obstruction

Bulldozer – right-of-way boat

Obstructions include shorelines, heavy patches of weed, fishing nets, shallows, moored boats, motor boats, crusing boats and, in some situations, other boats racing. Right-of-way boats and boats which refuse to give way, are out of control or capsized all rate as obstructions.

Mark

'A mark is any object specified in the sailing instructions which a yacht must round or pass on a required side. Every ordinary part of a mark ranks as part of it, including a flag, flagpole, boom or hoisted boat, but excluding ground tackle and any object either accidentally or temporarily attached to the mark'. (Definition.)

A dinghy tied to a mark does not count as part of the mark, unless specified in the sailing instructions (RYA appeal case 7 1971): nor does anything that has accidentally become attached to it or is only temporarily attached.

A mark's ground tackle is not counted as part of the mark (USYRU appeal No. 3), but when a boat runs into the mooring line and is drawn onto any part of the mark, above or below water, she is counted as having hit the mark (USYRU appeal No. 59).

Windward leg

A windward leg or, as it's often called, a beat, is a leg of the course which is sailed close-hauled, and on which the mark that ends the leg can not be reached without putting in at least one tack.

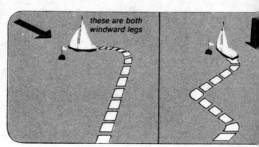

these are both windward legs

Offwind leg

Any leg which is not a windward leg is an offwind leg. A free leg (the rule book's term) or a downwind leg mean exactly the same.

Starting and finishing

Starting is dealt with at the beginning of the special section on starting (page 21) and finishing is dealt with at the beginning of the special section on finishing (page 79).

Postponement, abandonment and cancellation

A postponed race is one which is not started at its scheduled time and which can be sailed at any time the race committee may decide.

Abandonment and cancellation are often confused with one another because their special meanings as defined in the sailing rules are not those of everyday use. An abandoned race is one which the race committee calls off at any time after the start and which may be re-sailed at its discretion. A race which is cancelled before its scheduled start cannot be sailed. A race which is cancelled after it has been started cannot be re-sailed. A race officer usually abandons: the committee cancel or arrange a re-sail.

Collision

A collision happens when there is contact between any part of one boat (including all rigging, sails and sheets) or her crew and part of another boat or her crew.

Proper course

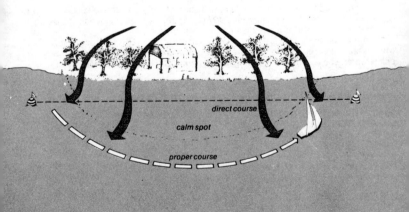

direct course

calm spot

proper course

direction
of next mark

*proper course for this boat,
as she surfs down a wave may
well be 15 or 20 degrees
low of the straight line
course to the next mark*

'A proper course is any course which a yacht might sail after the starting signal, in the absence of other yacht or yachts affected, to finish as quickly as possible . . .' (Definition.) The reference to other yacht or yachts affected means that a helmsman is not sailing his proper course if, for example, he bears away solely to gain a tactical advantage over a boat or boats just behind or overlapping him.

Proper course refers to the course the boat makes good and not the direction she is pointing (RYA case 9 1969 and USYRU Appeal No. 79).

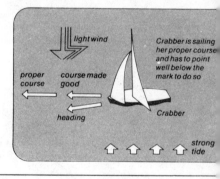

light wind

proper course

course made good

heading

Crabber is sailing her proper course and has to point well below the mark to do so

Crabber

There is no proper course before the starting signal.

strong tide

Helmsman

Someone of either sex who is steering a sailing boat. Referred to as he.

Yacht

The IYRU rule book uses the word 'yacht' to mean any sailing boat. In the official language of the rule book, sailboards, Optimists, Lasers and 505s, for example, are all yachts, though no-one who sails them would normally refer to them as yachts – except in jest.

THE START

The starting period covered in this section runs from the moment a boat receives her preparatory signal to the moment after the starting signal when she starts.

Timing of starts

A race is usually started by a 10 minute warning signal, a 5 minute preparatory signal and th start signal. If there is an error of timing between the 10 minute and 5 minute signals, the star ing signal must follow exactly 5 minutes after the preparatory signal – unless the race is the postponed (rule 4.4(d)). A national authority or a race committee through its sailing instruction may specify different timings. This often happens in team races where a 6 minute, 3 minut start sequence may be used (rule 4.4(a) and (b)).

The timing is taken from the visual signals, not from the sound signals (rule 4.5).

The racing rules come into force with the back-up of penalties at the 5 minute preparato signal (Definition of racing Part I of the rules).

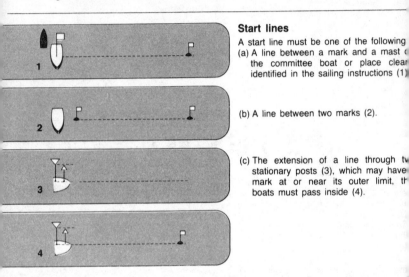

Start lines

A start line must be one of the following
(a) A line between a mark and a mast c the committee boat or place clear identified in the sailing instructions (1)

(b) A line between two marks (2).

(c) The extension of a line through tw stationary posts (3), which may have mark at or near its outer limit, th boats must pass inside (4).

On starting lines of types (1), (3) and (4) an inner distance mark, clearly defined in th sailing instructions, may be laid. Boats must then pass between this mark and the out distance mark. These floating marks should never be laid on the pre-start side of the lin (that is, behind the line) but always exactly on or just over it, otherwise they might r rate as starting marks when more than one boats-length behind the line.

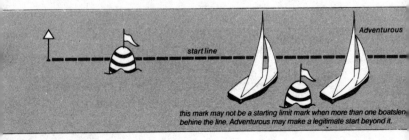

this mark may not be a starting limit mark when more than one boatslen behine the line. Adventurous may make a legitimate start beyond it.

er the line at the start

en any part of a boat, her sails, rigging, equipment or crew is on the course side of
 start line at the starting signal the boat is a premature starter (rule 8).

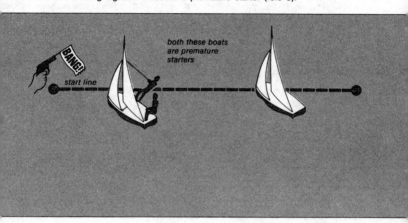

When one or more boats are premature starters, the race officer must make a sound sig-
 and display code flag 'X'.

A boat which has started prematurely must now re-start or be disqualified. But a prema-
e starter who does not realise her error is not required to go back and re-start when the
ual signal is not accompanied by the prescribed sound signal (rule 8.1 and IYRU case 70).

When a recalled boat has returned completely to the pre-start side of the start line, she
 start correctly. The 'X' flag is lowered once last of the premature starters has returned
he pre-start side of the line, or four minutes after the starting signal, whichever is the earlier
e 8.1).

Any boat anchored before the start with part of her ground tackle on the course side
the start line at the start signal becomes a premature starter because the anchor and
rp are part of the boat's equipment (rule 8.1).

When code flag 'I' has been displayed, any boat whose hull, equipment or crew is
 the course side of the start line during the minute before the start must sail round one
 of the line before starting. She may not just dip back over the line (rule 51.1(c)).

itting a starting mark

boat which collides with a starting mark after the preparatory signal can stay in the race pro-
Jed she immediately sails clear of other boats and makes two 360 degree turns (a '720').

20 degree penalty for an infringement before the start signal

'hen the sailing instructions specify that the 720 degree penalty is in force the turns must be
one at the first reasonable opportunity after the infringement. This usually means sailing clear
 other boats to find a space. (720 degree turns are dealt with in detail on pages 86–7.)

An infringement just before the starting signal will therefore result in a much more seve[re] penalty than an infringement soon after the preparatory signal.

If the infringement occurs before the wrong-doer has started (or if he is a premature st[ar]ter not yet returned) then the 720 must be done at the first reasonable opportunity, whichev[er] side of the line that happens to be. If at the end of doing the 720 he is on, or on the course si[de] of, the line he must go back behind the line and re-start.

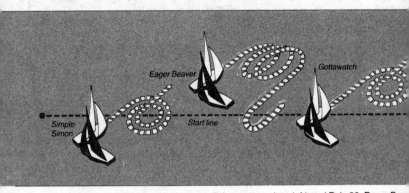

It is two seconds after the start and all these port tackers infringed Rule 36. Eager Bea[ver] was a premature starter and must go back to restart after completing the 720. Simple Sim[on] will also need to get behind the line after completing his turns because until he has taken [pe]nalty he can't start (definition of starting). Only Gottawatch can sail on after his 720 because [he] had started correctly before he infringed.

Anchored, moored, tied up or still ashore

A boat may be disqualified for being ashore, moored or tied up after the preparatory (5 minu[te]) signal (rule 53). If she doesn't sail about the vicinity of the start line between the preparat[ory] and starting signals or does not start, she is counted as a non-starter (rule 50 and IYRU ca[se] 34).

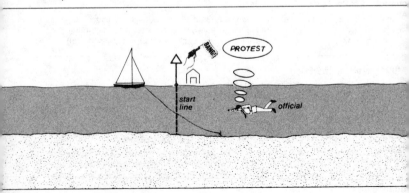

If she does get to the vicinity of the line before the starting signal, she must be ranked as a starter (rule 50) and can only be disqualified under rule 53 after a proper protest hearing. A helmsman cannot exonerate himself under this rule by taking any alternative penalties since they only apply to the right-of-way rules in Part IV of the rule book. Rule 53 is in Part V.

A boat may be anchored after the preparatory signal or held by a member of the crew standing in the water, and no rule is broken (rule 53). However, if an anchor is over the line at the start, the boat is reckoned to be a premature starter.

no rule is broken by either of these boats

General recall

When the race officer can't pick out all the premature starters, or when the start is unsatisfactory in some other way, he can abandon the start by flying the First Substitute and making two more sound signals after the starting signal.

The procedure for the re-start is then:
First Substitute is lowered to the accompaniment of a sound signal.
After one minute a new preparatory signal is made.

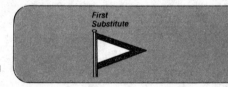

First Substitute

Once again, though, the sailing instructions may give a different procedure. This would have precedence over the IYRU standard procedure.

Any boat which commits a foul on the abandoned start is not barred from competing in any subsequent starts unless the sailing instructions specifically say so (and that is very rare except in unmanageably large starts) (rule 8.2.(b)).

Postponement

A race may be postponed by flying the Answering Pendant. The race will then be started after the scheduled time at the discretion of the race committee. The warning signal is made one minute after the Answering Pendant is lowered, accompanied by a sound signal.

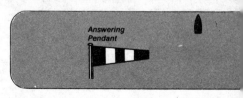

Answering Pendant

RIGHT OF WAY

Starting

A boat starts when any part of her hull, crew or equipment first crosses the start li
after the start signal in the direction of the first mark, provided she has no pena
obligations to fulfil. (Definition of starting in Part I of the rules.)

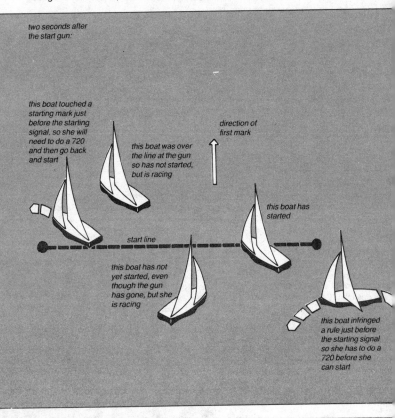

two seconds after the start gun:

this boat touched a starting mark just before the starting signal, so she will need to do a 720 and then go back and start

this boat was over the line at the gun so has not started, but is racing

direction of first mark

this boat has started

start line

this boat has not yet started, even though the gun has gone, but she is racing

this boat infringed a rule just before the starting signal so she has to do a 720 before she can start

No room at a starting mark

When approaching the line to start a windward boat (white) is not entitled to dema
room from any leeward boat (black) at a starting mark (rule 42.4).

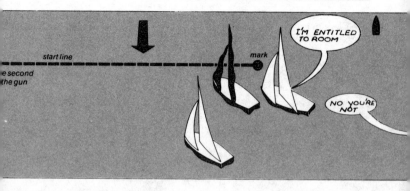

But after the starting signal the leeward boat is not entitled to squeeze the windward boat out at the mark by sailing either:

- above (that is, upwind of) the course to the first mark *or*
- above close-hauled (rule 42.4).

The mark must be a starting mark and surrounded by navigable water for this ruling to apply.

In the to-ing and fro-ing before the start, though, a windward boat is entitled to room at a starting mark, but only if it's an obstruction. The 'no water' rule applies only 'when approaching the line to start'.

At the other end of the start line, if there is just a small buoy, the leeward boat is not entitled to room (rule 42.4 and). The black boat here may only luff, slowly, above close hauled, if the white boat is not 'mast abeam' and is able to respond.

The position is quite different if the starting mark cannot be sailed round or th[e] line's length is limited by, say, a pier. A windward boat is then entitled to room at th[e] mark or pier (rule 42.4 does not apply; rule 42.1(a) does).

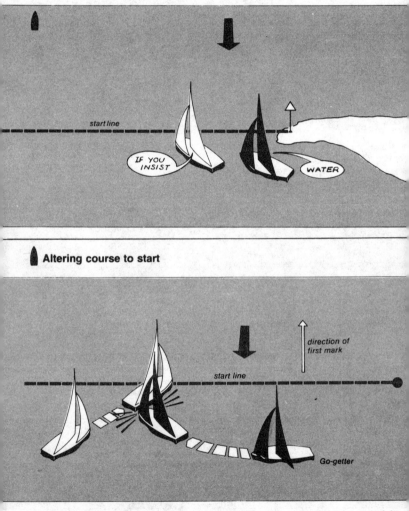

Altering course to start

A boat which is altering course to start does not have to worry about any non-right-o[f] way boats which are on the opposite tack, whereas at any other time in the race (exce[pt] at marks) she would (rule 35(b)(i)).

Go-getter is altering course to start and white is in the wrong. If she were not starting, **Go-getter,** as right-of-way boat, would be in the wrong for altering course in a way that obstructs a boat which was keeping clear.

Luffing before the start

The luffing rules that apply before a boat starts are fundamentally different from those that apply later. A luff may not be fast before she starts and the acquisition of luffing rights is quite different.

After the preparatory signal (5 minute) but before she has started and cleared the start line:

1. She may luff a windward boat slowly and in such a way that the windward boat has 'room and opportunity to keep clear' (rule 40).

2. The leeward boat has the right to luff as high as head to wind (again slowly) when the windward boat is aft of the mast abeam position – regardless of how the two boats came together (rule 40).

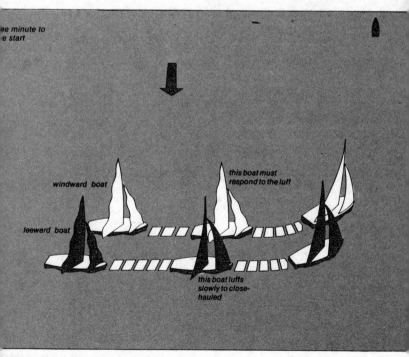

one minute to the start

windward boat

leeward boat

this boat must respond to the luff

this boat luffs slowly to close-hauled

The windward boat has not dropped behind the 'mast abeam' position (explained on page 72), so the leeward boat may not luff above close-hauled.

29

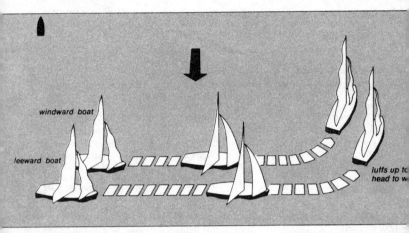

windward boat

leeward boat

luffs up to head to w

The leeward boat here is entitled to carry on luffing slowly until she is head to wind – provided the windward boat doesn't gain the 'mast abeam' position or move forward of it and provided the windward boat has 'room and opportunity to keep clear' (rules 40 and 38.2(c)).

If, for example, the windward boat was idling when the luff began, she would require time to gather way and respond to the luff. The leeward boat has to give her this opportunity. It is important to remember that the first movement of the windward boat's stern in responding to a luff is inevitably *towards* the leeward boat. The windward boat would not be disqualified in a pre-start luffing incident if she made every reasonable effort to avoid the leeward boat's luff from the moment the luff began.

3. A luff which is higher than close-hailed can be stopped by the windward helmsman if he reaches the 'mast abeam' position. He simply hails 'mast abeam' and the leeward boat must stop luffing and hold her course or bear away (rules 40 and 38.2(c)).

4. When more than one boat is overlapped upwind the leeward boat may not luff higher than close-hailed unless she has the right to luff *all* the overlapped boats head to wind (rules 40 and 38.2(e)).

5. A windward helmsman can hail to stop the leeward boat luffing when he can't respond because of an obstruction (rules 40 and 38.2(d)). A starting mark surrounded by navigable water does not rate as a legitimate obstruction when starting to leeward of it.

Over the line at the start

While a premature starter is sailing the course, she carries full rights. But at the moment she begins her manoeuvre to return, she loses the protection of the main right-of-way rules (rule 44).

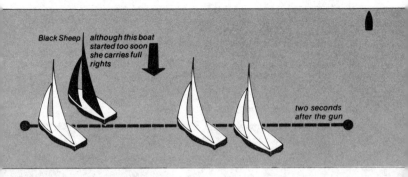

Now **Black Sheep** lets her sails flap to slow down. Her manoeuvre to return has begun and she must keep clear of all other boats (rule 44).

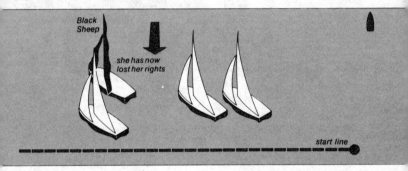

Once back on the pre-start side of the line **Black Sheep** gets back her rights, but she cannot make use of them immediately. She must allow boats over which she has right-of-way 'ample room and opportunity to keep clear' (rule 44.1(b)).

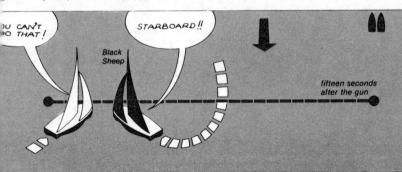

Black Sheep has acted too fast in claiming starboard rights. She has not given the port tack boat enough opportunity to keep clear. On this showing, **Black Sheep's** return to the fold would only be temporary.

When code flag 'I' has been displayed, any boat whose hull, equipment or crew on the course side of the start line or its extensions during the minute before the start must sail round one end of the line to start. She may not just dip back over the start line (rule 51.1(c)). The sailing instructions, though, may override this rule.

Starting from the wrong side of the line

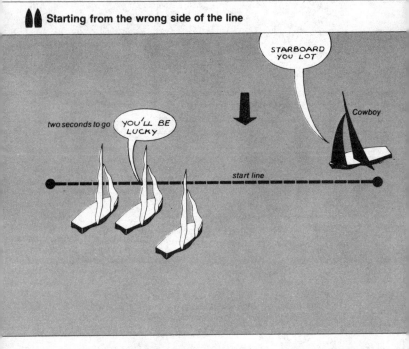

Cowboy enjoys right-of-way for 2 seconds more, then loses it as soon as the gun goes if she is caught with any part of the boat or crew on the wrong side of the line at the gun (rule 51.1(b) and 44.1(a)). If she gets behind the line in 2 seconds she has the right to head up and start as explained in 'Altering course to start', page 28.

But look out for any special starting provisions in the sailing instructions; they may override the IYRU rules that apply here.

Overtaking to leeward

This is very common before and at the start, though the rules that apply are much the same as would apply at any other time in the race.

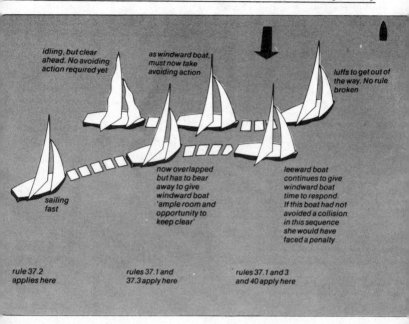

idling, but clear ahead. No avoiding action required yet

as windward boat, must now take avoiding action

luffs to get out of the way. No rule broken

sailing fast

now overlapped but has to bear away to give windward boat 'ample room and opportunity to keep clear'

leeward boat continues to give windward boat time to respond. If this boat had not avoided a collision in this sequence she would have faced a penalty.

rule 37.2 applies here

rules 37.1 and 37.3 apply here

rules 37.1 and 3 and 40 apply here

Ample room and opportunity (rule 37.3) means more than just sufficient, and the benefit of any doubt must go to the windward boat.

The one big difference in the overtaking rights-of-way before and after starting is in the rights of the leeward boat to luff (pages 30 and 72).

Overtaking a wayless boat

The wayless boat is an obstruction to **Rapide. Wayless** need not begin to take avoiding action until **Rapide** overlaps. Therefore the initial avoiding action must be by **Rapide**. Any boat overlapped to leeward of **Rapide (Oblivious)** must keep clear if she's to avoid penalty – even when **Rapide** fails to call 'water' and **Oblivious'** crew doesn't see the wayless boat (rules 37.3 and 42.1(a) and USYRU Appeal No. 46).

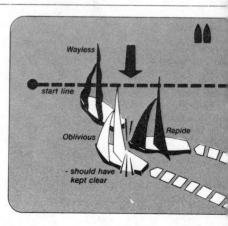

Wayless

start line

Oblivious

Rapide

- should have kept clear

WINDWARD LEG

A windward leg is one that a
boat can complete only by
putting in at least one tack.

OPPOSITE TACKS

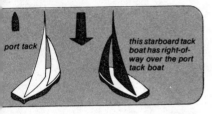

Port and starboard

A port tack boat gives way to a starboard tack boat (rule 36).

When there is no collision and a close-hauled starboard tack boat bears away to miss the port boat's stern, the onus of proof is on the port tack helmsman to show that the starboard boat would have missed had she held her course (RYA case 1 1973, USYRU case 32 and IYRU case 113).

The port tack helmsman may hail 'hold your course' but this hail is not binding on the starboard boat, which can still bear away to miss and protest (USYRU case 137). In dinghies, though, it is no bad thing for the starboard helmsman to hold his course in these circumstances. A rudder or transom clipped saves any argument.

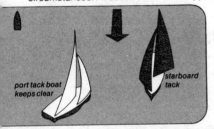

A starboard tack boat sailing free has right-of-way over a close-hauled port tack boat, so long as the starboard tacker does not alter course in a way that prevents the port tack boat keeping clear (rules 35 and 36).

Port and starboard when the starboard tack boat alters course

A port and starboard incident where the starboard tack boat alters course and hits – or claims she could have hit – a port tacker is quite different from the straight-forward port and starboard case above. This situation is controlled by rule 35, which is designed to deny *carte blanche* to alter course and hit give way boats.

The white boat on starboard is in the wrong because she altered course when the port boat was properly keeping clear. Nor can an offwind starboard tack boat legitimately alter course to hit a port tack boat that is sailing a course to keep clear.

Even when there is a windshift, rule 35 can override the basic port and starboard rule (IYRU case 52, RYA case 5 1974 and USYRU case 157). To use the windshift as a defence at a protest hearing, black would have to establish to the committee's satisfaction that she was clearly going to cross white before the windshift complicated matters.

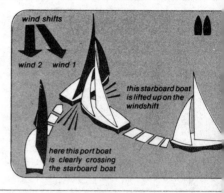

wind shifts

wind 2   wind 1

this starboard boat is lifted up on the windshift

here this port boat is clearly crossing the starboard boat

Port and starboard when starboard tack boat has just tacked

'A yacht shall neither tack nor gybe into a position which will give her right of way unless she does so far enough from a yacht on a tack to enable this yacht to keep clear without having to begin to alter her course until after the tack or gybe has been completed' (rule 41.2).

The boat which has just tacked (**Jack-in-the-box**) has the onus of satisfying the race committee that the tack was completed far enough from the other boat (rule 41.3). Protest committees are too often apt to place the onus on the port tack boat, merely because the port and starboard rule is basic. In cases like this one they would be wrong to do that.

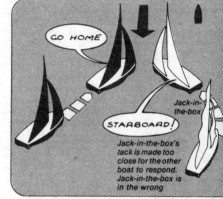

GO HOME

STARBOARD!

Jack-in-the-box

Jack-in-the-box's tack is made too close for the other boat to respond. Jack-in-the-box is in the wrong

Calling 'starboard'

There is no obligation to call 'starboard', but anybody who makes a habit of not hailing would soon become pretty unpopular – particularly when tacking onto starboard a few lengths away from a port tack boat.

The starboard tack boat on the right breaks no rule by hailing 'starboard', putting the port tack boat about, then tacking.

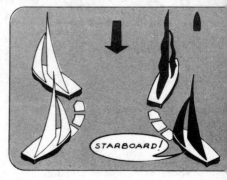

STARBOARD!

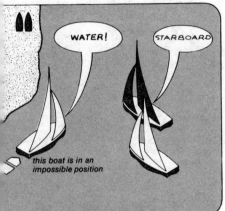

this boat is in an impossible position

Opposite tack boat requiring room for an obstruction

There is, curiously, no way that a port tack boat which is prevented from tacking by an obstruction can legitimately force starboard tack boats to tack and give her room. Only when she calls for room before tacking onto port can she put the starboard tackers about without infringing the rules (rule 43, explained opposite). Otherwise the port and starboard rule (36) applies, in spite of the fact that the port tack boat's only escape may be to bear away hard or go aground.

SAME TACK

Windward and leeward

When two boats are beating on the same tack and the one to windward is not sailing as close to the wind as the leeward one, the windward boat must keep clear (rule 37.1)

windward boat

The leeward boat may not sail above her proper course (close-hauled here) unless she has luffing rights (rule 38.1 and 38.2(a)).

If the leeward boat has come up from clear astern, she must allow the windward boat 'ample room and opportunity to keep clear' from the moment the overlap is established (rule 37.3). This may mean that the leeward boat has to bear off initially, but the windward boat is required to respond by luffing above her close hauled course if necessary. Again, the initial onus to keep clear is on the boat which has newly acquired right-of-way (the leeward one).

The crew or helmsman of the leeward boat may not deliberately reach out, sit out or trapeze with the prime intention of hitting the windward boat (RYA case 6 1971). This is penalised under the fair sailing rule.

Luffing

The rule is exactly the same as for an off-wind leg (page 72). I should mention one situation, though, which only crops up on the beat; it represents a particularly sharp, but legitimate, use of the luffing rule.

From the moment the leeward boat completes a tack a new set of rights comes in (rule 38.2(b)). And if the leeward boat has luffing rights when she completes her tack, then once she's given the windward boat an opportunity to keep clear, she may luff as sharply as she likes, up to head to wind (rules 41.2 and 38.1). Though she is not entitled to cause serious damage (rule 32.)

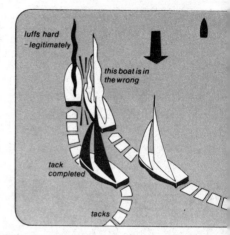

luffs hard
– legitimately

this boat is in
the wrong

tack
completed

tacks

Bearing down

Provided the leeward boat isn't made to alter course to avoid hitting the windward boat, the windward boat may bear away below close-hauled as white does here.

This would not be allowed on an offwind leg because rule 39 (sailing below a proper course) forbids it, but that rule applies only to free legs, not beats. It is also worth remembering that it is the leg itself that counts, not the actual point of sailing, so if two boats have overstood a weather mark the windward one may bear down on the other since, although sailing free, they are still on the windward leg. (A windward leg is defined on page 17.)

DONT BEAR
DOWN ANY
MORE

Calling for room at a continuous obstruction

If **Mud Tickler** carries on she'll hit the shore; if she tacks she'll hit white. The rules provide a way out of this one provided both boats are on the same tack as they are here: **Mud Tickler** can hail 'water',

Mud
Tickler

shore

WATER

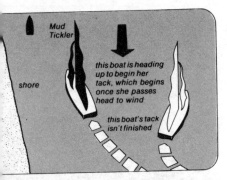

'shore room' or something similar a white before tacking. (But if she makes the call after tacking she'll be in trouble as explained on page 38).

The white boat here must now respond either by immediately:

1. tacking *or*
2. hailing 'you tack' (rule 43.2(b)).

If white chooses to tack, **Mud Tickler** must begin to tack immediately she is able to tack and clear the white boat (rule 43.2(a) and USYRU case 108). But **Mud Tickler** is not entitled to hail and tack simultaneously into white (rule 43.1).

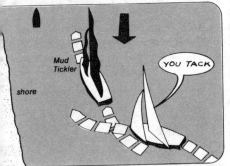

White may prefer to let **Mud Tickler** tack, keep out of her way and really squeeze into the shore herself. The white must call 'you tack' and avoid **Mud Tickler.** The onus is now entirely on white to keep out of the way (rule 43.2(b)(ii) and (iii)).

Once white has made her 'you tack' call, **Mud Tickler** must tack immediately. If she doesn't she can be protested against – even if there is no collision (rule 43. (b)(i)).

The commonest problems in these situations come up when short tacking against a tide, and hinge on how far apart the boats need to be before the inshore boat's call for water is invalid. There is no set number of boat lengths – the distance will vary according to the conditions and the type of boat – but the criteria for deciding are quite clear. The inshore boat is not entitled to hail for water when:

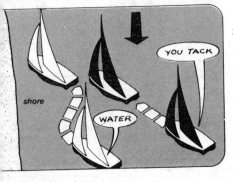

1. she can tack out from the shore and back again onto her original tack without tacking in the other boat's water *or*
2. she can tack and bear off behind the other boat without difficulty.

The white boat here is able to tack out from the shore and back onto her original tack without tacking in black's water. White's hail was therefore illegal. Black must still respond to the hail (for example by hailing 'you tack') and may then protest. However, if the protest committee is satisfied that it was reasonable for white to believe she could not tack with the possibility of not being able to keep clear of black, then white's hail will be ruled as valid, even though, as it turned out here, white was in fact able to keep clear of black after completing her tack onto port.

In this sequence, white's call was dubious, but since she believed she was going to find it difficult to tack and clear black, she had the right to hail.

Black took a chance by hailing 'you tack' but, as it turned out, white was able to tack and bear off behind black without difficulty, so there was no infringement (rule 43.1 and USYRU case 108).

Calling for room at a non-continuous obstruction

A non-continuous obstruction is one which can be passed on either side and requires a boat not less than a length away to make a substantial alteration of course to miss it. Moored boats, miniscule islands, capsized boats, other boats sailing and motor boats may all be non-continuous obstructions (the definition is on page 17).

Once the 'water' call has been made here by black, white must respond exactly as in the section above (rule 43). The fact that white would have missed the obstruction anyway doesn't matter. Nor does it matter that black chose to tack rather than bear off and go to leeward of the obstruction. There is no rule which dictates that a boat should take the shortest route around an obstruction. Although if black would only need to make a small alteration of course when one length away, the rules don't allow her to call for water to tack; she must then make the course change, staying on the same tack (USYRU case 81).

A starboard tack boat as an obstruction

One of the commonest obstructions to sea room is a starboard tack boat. Usually it will be close-hauled but it can be running free.

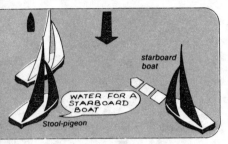

Stool-pigeon is entitled to hail f
water to tack, and the white boat mu
either tack immediately or call 'you tac
Stool-pigeon has to see this situatio
coming in good time or she'll be too la
to call and won't be able to get out of t
starboard tacker's way (rule 43 and defi
tion of an obstruction).

When **Stool-pigeon** calls clearly for room to tack in good time, and white fails t
respond, the responsibility is entirely white's and no blame falls on **Stool-pigeo**
for white's failure to tack. (As USYRU case 142 conflicts with IYRU case 6 here, I hav
taken the IYRU interpretation since, though earlier, it will apply everywhere outside th
United States.)

Instead of tacking, **Stool-pigeon** can choose to bear away astern of the starboa
boat, since an obstruction can be taken on either side; but she must then give any roo
white might need if she needs to take action to avoid the starboard boat and wishes to g
underneath (rule 42.1(a) and definition of obstruction).

If white asks for water to bear off behind the starboard boat at the same moment as **Stoo**
pigeon asks for room to tack, **Stool-pigeon**'s call governs. White only gets room if **Stoo**
pigeon chooses not to hail for room to tack, in which case **Stool-pigeon** must give roo
whether or not white hails (USYRU case 131).

🔺🔺 Forcing another boat to overstand a weather mark

The team racing ploy of holding an opponent on the same tack to sail beyond the lay line ar
overstand the weather mark is explained on page 64.

TACKING

Tacking in the water of a starboard tack boat

A boat which is tacking is required to keep clear of a boat which is not tacking (rule 41). Tacking is explained on page 15.

Even when the tacking boat has completed her tack she is not necessarily in the clear. Any nearby boat on a tack has no need to alter course to avoid her until her tack is complete – that is, until her boom is across and she is heading on a close-hauled course (though her sails needn't be filling).

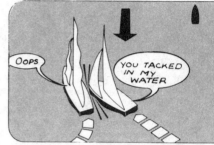

In a protest, the onus is on the boat that tacks to satisfy the race committee that she did so far enough ahead to allow the boat already on the tack to keep clear (rule 41.3 and RYA case 3 1970). In a close tacking incident the boat which is tacking can often help to establish the facts to the satisfaction of a protest committee by calling at the time, 'I'm round now', then counting steadily 1,2,3,4... and stopping when either there's a collision or the other boat overlaps. In spite of the onus of proof, it is possible to tack quite close from port to starboard without breaking any rules.

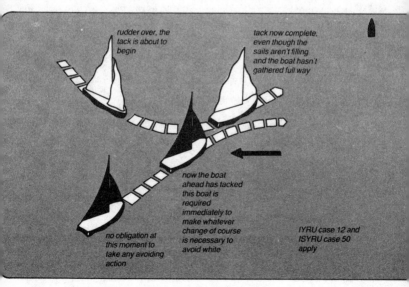

rudder over, the tack is about to begin

tack now complete, even though the sails aren't filling and the boat hasn't gathered full way

now the boat ahead has tacked this boat is required immediately to make whatever change of course is necessary to avoid white

no obligation at this moment to take any avoiding action

IYRU case 12 and ISYRU case 50 apply

Tacking in the water of a port tack boat

It is not possible to tack as close to another boat when going from starboard tack to port as it is in going from port to starboard.

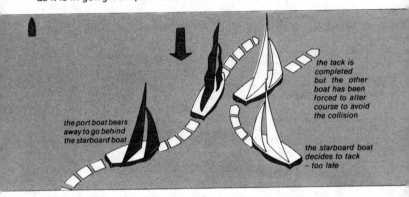

the tack is completed but the other boat has been forced to alter course to avoid the collision

the port boat bears away to go behind the starboard boat

the starboard boat decides to tack – too late

White is in the wrong under rule 35 – which is the one that bars a right-of-way boat from altering course when a give way boat is sailing a course to keep clear. For white to be in the wrong here under rule 35 a protest committee must establish that the port tack boat (black) began to bear off to go behind white before white had altered course to tack.

Once black has borne off, the situation is treated as a close-hauled boat (white) tacking in front of a close reaching boat (black) and the tacking in water rule (41) applies.

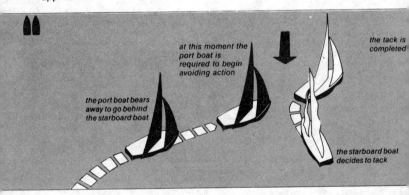

at this moment the port boat is required to begin avoiding action

the tack is completed

the port boat bears away to go behind the starboard boat

the starboard boat decides to tack

At the moment white's tack is completed, black must take whatever avoiding action, including going head to wind, necessary to avoid white. In practice, the port tack boat would head up back to close-hauled as soon as the other boat was seen to be tacking; but for the purposes of deciding a case like this in protest, premature avoiding action by black would not automatically exonerate the tacking boat (rule 41.3).

Simultaneous tacking

When two boats are tacking at the same time, the one on the other's port side keeps clear (rule 41.4).

The easy way to remember simultaneous tacking or gybing onus is quoted in *Elvström Explains* – 'If you're on the right, you're in the right'.

The rule does allow Black's helmsman to wait for the other boat's helm to go down and then put his own down, since tacking only happens from the moment a boat goes past head to wind until she is pointing on the new close-hauled course. This takes a little time. As long as the tacking of each boat coincides, they are defined as tacking simultaneously (USYRU case 129). In dinghies and small keel-boats it can be risky to tack immediately after crossing close ahead of a port tack boat – especially if the port tack boat has borne away to miss the starboard tacker's stern, since she'll be moving extra fast into any tack she might make.

MARK ROUNDING

The mark-rounding rules come into effect when a boat is 'about to round the mark', and continue until the mark is left astern.

Where the mark-rounding rules come into force

The special rules which apply to rounding marks and obstructions are in Part IV Section C of the IYRU rules. Rules of that section override rules of Section B with which they conflict. For simplicity's sake here I have dealt separately with mark-rounding. Obstructions are dealt with in the sections on windward legs and offwind legs.

The mark-rounding rules come into force when the leading boat of the pair (or bunch) is 'about to round' the mark. This is usually at two boat-lengths but in heavy seas or with a tidal stream increasing the boat's speed over the ground, or when the boats are fast catamarans, or

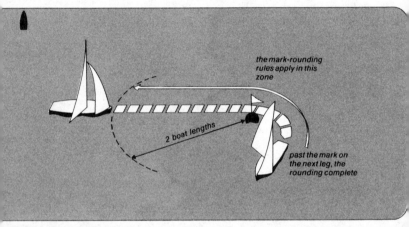

A boat overlapped on another which is already in the two lengths circle is also governed by the mark-rounding rules (42.1).

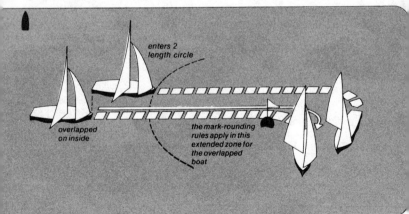

when a big bunch of boats is coming together at the mark, this distance could be much more. The mark-rounding rules apply until the mark has been rounded or passed (rule 42.3(a)).

The most usual cases where the zone in which the mark-rounding rules apply can extend further back than two lengths are when:

1. Several boats are overlapped
   The outside boats are required to give room as the boats are 'about to round the mark' (rule 42). Which may mean giving room well before the two lengths circle.
   or
2. A leading boat is physically incapable of giving room. For example, a multi-hull travelling fast (in boats other than multi-hulls this special provision, rule 42.3(a)(i), is rarely used).

The penalty for hitting a mark

A boat is exonerated for hitting a mark if she does a '720'; that is, sails well clear of all other boats as soon as possible and remains clear while making two complete 360 turns in the same direction, including two tacks and two gybes.

A boat is counted as hitting a mark when any part of her hull, crew or equipment touches it. So a neat hand-off or a spinnaker sheet touching a flag on the mark is a touch (rule 52 and definition of a mark). The mark's mooring line or chain is not counted as part of the mark (definition again) – though the crew may not use the mooring line to stop the boat touching the mark (rule 54).

When a boat hits the 'wrong' side of a mark (sails the wrong side of it and hits it) she must first go off and do her 720, and then come back and round it on the right side.

Forced onto a mark by another boat

When a boat is forced onto a mark through, her helmsman believes, a rule infringement by another boat, the helmsman need not take any penalty for hitting the mark provided he protests (rule 52). He can either accept his penalty for hitting the mark and not protest against the other boat, or lodge a protest against this other boat, or both. If the protest committee finds that the collision with the mark was a result of an infringement by the other boat, the collision with the mark is forgiven and the other boat disqualified. However, if the offending boat immediately retires (or does a 720) the mark hitter may sail on without taking a penalty. If the offending yacht does not retire (or do a 720) the mark hitter must protest (rule 52.1(b)(i)).

In the rare event of a mark being submerged by a boat sailing over it, then shooting out of the water to hit a following boat, this boat need not be penalised. She can't protest against the mark, but she can protest against the boat that caused its irregular behaviour. However, she is still obliged to go the correct side of it, no matter where it surfaces (IYRU case 18).

Rights of a boat which has just hit a mark

It can happen that a boat misjudges the course to a mark, hits it and then collides with another boat over which, ignoring the brush with the mark, she would have had right-of-way. What are her rights after touching the mark?

She keeps all her rights until she is 'well clear' of other boats, at which time she no longer needs them because she is 'well clear'. As soon as she touches the mark, in addition to any normal obligations she might have (like port tack keeps clear of starboard tack) she is, of course, obligated to sail well clear of all other boats as soon as possible, but she does keep her rights while sailing clear.

Rounding a mark in the wrong direction

After rounding a mark the wrong way, the mistake can be corrected by unwinding. To do this correctly, a string representing the boat's wake would, when drawn tight, have to lie on the required side of the mark (rule 51.2 and 51.4). You don't lose any rights, just because you're going back to unwind or are in the process of unwinding.

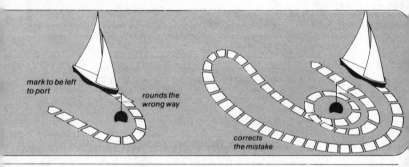

mark to be left to port

rounds the wrong way

corrects the mistake

A mark is only a mark of the course for the leg it defines

A mark is only a mark of the course for a particular boat when it defines the leg of the course which that boat is sailing (rule 52.1(a)(ii)). So on leg 5 - 1 mark 1 is a mark of the course and may not be hit without penalty, but on leg 3 - 4 mark 1 can be hit without penalty.

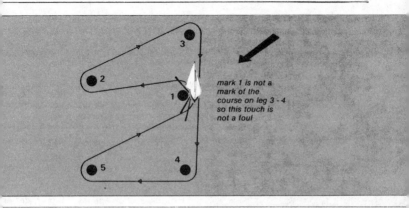

mark 1 is not a
mark of the
course on leg 3 - 4
so this touch is
not a foul

Mark missing or moved

The race committee should return a drifting mark to its stated position if possible.
If that isn't possible they must replace it by
a new one with 'similar characteristics' or
a buoy or boat displaying the letter M of
the International Code (rule 9.1(a)). Failing that, the race must be shortened,
cancelled, abandoned or postponed (rule
9.1(b)).

ROUNDING AT THE END OF AN OFFWIND LEG

Room at a mark

A boat which is overlapped on others outside
her has the right to room at the mark, provided the overlap is established before the
leading boat enters an imaginary circle round
the mark whose diameter is two of the leading boat's lengths and provided that when the
inside boat establishes the overlap the outside boat is able to give room (rules 42.1(a)
and 3(a)(ii)). The explanation of an overlap is
on page 16.

If the leading boat is unable to give
room, the inside boat is not entitled to it (rule
42.3(a)(i)). In other words she is not expected to do the impossible. Situations in
which the leading boat is unable to give room
are rare in monohulls but include:

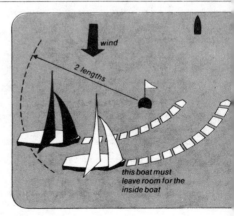

this boat must
leave room for the
inside boat

1. Situations where groups of boats in the line abreast simply cannot shift aside fast enough to accommodate a late inside overlapper – even though her overlap may have been established outside the two lengths circle.
2. High speed planing or surfing, when the leading boat just isn't able to respond fast enough two lengths from the mark to let anyone in.

The onus of proof here would be with the boat claiming room.

Circumstances where a helmsman isn't able to give room because he isn't properly in control of his boat are not included: a helmsman's incompetence or inexperience is no defence (RYA case 4 1975).

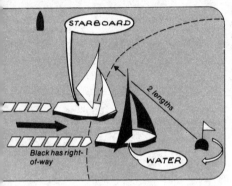

Black has right-of-way

Port and starboard at an offwind m

The rights of the inside boat take preference over the port and starboard rights as the note under Section C of the rule book (Part IV) makes clear: 'When a rule of this section applies ... it overrides any conflicting rule of Part IV which precedes it'. The port and starboard rule precedes it.

Before the leader enters the two lengths circle, of course, the starboard boat (white) has right-of-way (rule 36).

The onus in establishing an overlap

A boat which comes from clear astern to claim an inside overlap has the onus of satisfying a protest committee (if the argument gets that far) that the overlap was established in proper time (rule 42.1(d)).

Pusher would find it very difficult to establish that her inside overlap was made soon enough. A witness in another boat or ashore might clinch it, but even so **Pusher** would be foolish in this situation to round on the inside and risk near-certain disqualification. If the outside boat readily concedes the overlap, that's a different matter; then **Pusher** is entitled to round inside.

The onus in breaking an overlap

When two overlapped boats are approaching a mark and just before entering the two lengths circle the outside one claims that she has broken the overlap, she has the onus of satisfying any protest committee that she had become clear ahead before entering the two lengths circle (rule 42.1(c)).

If the inside boat – which doesn't have the onus of proof – strongly disputes a marginal 'clear ahead' claim at the time, the outside helmsman would be stupid to try and push his luck by going for the inside berth.

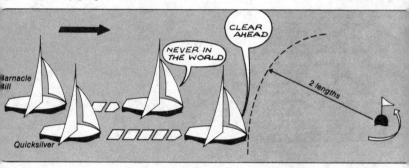

The onus of proof that the overlap has been broken is on **Quicksilver**, who would be foolish to go for the inside berth unless she could be sure **Barnacle Bill** would not have to avoid her during the rounding.

Hailing for water

The rules don't insist on a hail, but a hail that the overlap is either established or broken helps to support the claim (rule 42.1(f)). An overlap which is established well before the two lengths circle and is not marginal needs no hail for water from the inside boat.

How overlaps operate when boats are making a wide rounding

In a big fleet it often happens at a leeward mark that boats round very wide at the end of a downwind leg so that they come in close to the mark for a good start to the following leg. If a boat goes so wide that she enters the two lengths circle at right angles to the oncoming fleet, the whole fleet is entitled to water – they are forward of the line at right angles to her aftermost point. They won't all be able to make use of their right, but some might be able to, as **Interloper** can on the white boat.

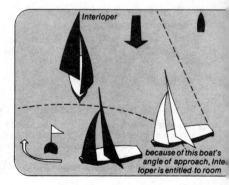

because of this boat's angle of approach, Interloper is entitled to room

How overlaps operate when a boat is carried past a mark by a tide

A boat which enters the two lengths circle and leaves it has to establish her overlap rights anew when she re-enters the circle (IRYU case 71).

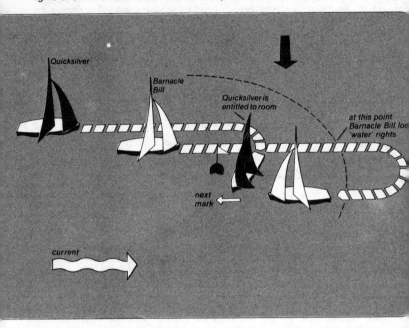

Quicksilver

Barnacle Bill

Quicksilver is entitled to room

at this point Barnacle Bill loses 'water' rights

next mark ←

current →

The same principle applies in really windy conditions when a skipper chooses to tack round instead of gybe and during his tack sails past the mark and outside the two lengths circle. He must establish new rights on re-entering the circle.

Tacking at a mark

When one boat is clear ahead of another and a tack is an integral part of the rounding – as, say, from a reach to a reach – the rules that apply are exactly the same as in the section on rounding at the end of windward legs (page 62). When a boat tacks instead of gybes because it's a bit windy, the tacking in water rules still apply and the overlap conditions are identical to those explained in the section above.

How much room an inside boat is allowed

An inside boat with another overlapped outside her is not entitled to round as wide as she likes within the two lengths circle. To quote rule 42.1(a): 'Room is the space needed by an inside overlapping yacht, that is handled in a seamanlike manner in the prevailing conditions, to pass in safety between an outside yacht and a mark or obstruction'. This includes room to tack or gybe when either is an integral part of the rounding manoeuvre.

54

This definition makes white's rounding here, in which the outside boat is pushed wide for purely tactical reasons, very risky. The dividing line between what is purely a 'seamanlike' rounding and a rounding made primarily for maximum tactical gain is a fine one. The onus of proof here lies with the outside boat to establish that the inside boat has gone unduly wide. In this situation black would win the protest. One and a half lengths here is too wide; one length would probably not be.

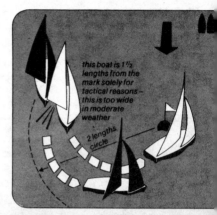

this boat is 1½ lengths from the mark solely for tactical reasons – this is too wide in moderate weather

2 lengths circle

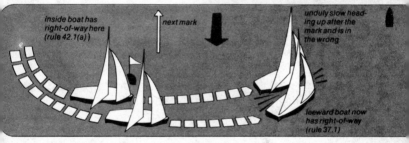

inside boat has right-of-way here (rule 42.1(a))

next mark

unduly slow heading up after the mark and is in the wrong

leeward boat now has right-of-way (rule 37.1)

Once the mark has been passed, the inside boat's right under the mark-rounding rules end and the right-of-way rules that apply for a leg of the course come into play (IYRU case 50).

Breaking an overlap inside the two lengths circle

An outside boat which is required to give room because of an overlap made before entering the two lengths circle is still required to give room if the overlap is subsequently broken (rule 42.1(b)).

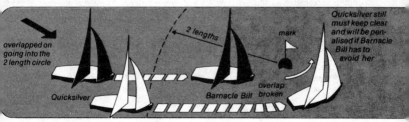

overlapped on going into the 2 length circle

2 lengths

mark

Quicksilver still must keep clear and will be penalised if Barnacle Bill has to avoid her

Quicksilver

Barnacle Bill

overlap broken

Gybing at a mark
There is no such infringement as gybing in someone's water at a mark after starting (rule 42.2(a)).

Inside boat required to gybe at the first opportunity
An inside boat must gybe at the first reasonable opportunity when a gybe is necessary to get on to the proper course for the next leg, except when the inside boat has luffing rights (rule 42.1(e)).

When the inside boat has luffing rights there is no need for her to gybe. In fact, the inside boat may luff at any time or just sail straight past the mark (rule 42.1(e) does not now apply; rule 38.1 does).

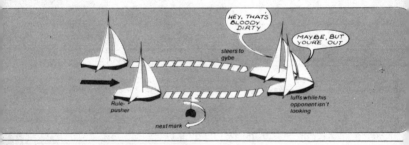

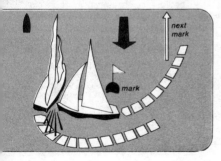

Rounding onto a beat
The port tack boat is in the wrong here, in spite of the right-of-way starboard tack boat altering course. The rule which forbids alteration of course in a way that prevents another boat keeping clear (rule 35) specifically makes an exception of a right-of-way boat rounding a mark. The port and starboard rule (36) governs (USYRU case 167).

Luffing another boat the wrong side of a mark

Luffing another boat the wrong side of a mark is rarely wise in normal fleet racing but is some-times a good tactic in team racing when, by luffing one of the opposition the wrong side of a mark, a team-mate is able to slip by.

There used to be a rule (rule 42.3(c)) which required a hail by the luffing boat when within the vicinity of the mark, and prohibiting the manoeuvre when within two lengths of the mark.

Now the rule has been removed:

(a) No hail is required by the luffing boat,
(b) there is no point past which the luffing boat must take the windward boat, and
(c) a leeward boat may not luff a windward boat the wrong side of the mark, once the leading boat is 'about to round' the mark. It is difficult to determine exactly when a yacht is 'about to round', but it would be rare for this to be less than two lengths, and it could often be more (IYRU case 55).

So for a boat to be allowed to luff another boat the wrong side of the mark:
(a) the leeward boat must have luffing rights, and
(b) the leading boat must not be about to round the mark.

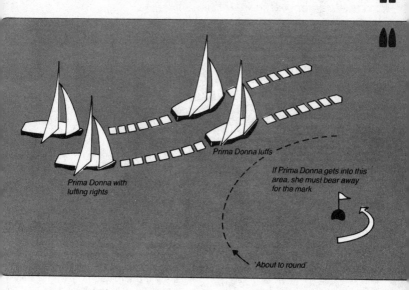

Prima Donna luffs

If Prima Donna gets into this area, she must bear away for the mark

Prima Donna with luffing rights

'About to round'

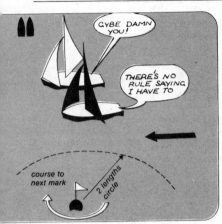

Using starboard rights to sail a boat the wrong side of a mark

When two boats are on opposite tacks the starboard boat may sail any course and the port boat must keep clear (rule 36 and IYRU case 17). This means that provided both boats remain well outside the two lengths circle the starboard boat may sail the port boat the wrong side of the mark. No hail is necessary but any alteration of course by the starboard tack boat towards the port-tack boat must be slow to avoid infringing rule 35 (IYRU case 35).

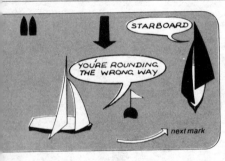

Rounding a mark in opposite directions

When boats are rounding a mark in opposite directions the port and starboard rule (36) applies even though the starboard boat is rounding the wrong way (IYRU case 37). When a boat is 'unwinding' because she sailed round the mark the wrong way, she maintains her rights.

ROUNDING AT THE END OF A WINDWARD LEG

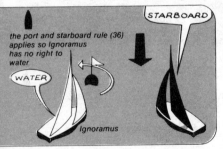

On opposite tacks – port and starboard

When boats on opposite tacks are about to round a windward mark the rules apply essentially as though there were no mark there (rule 42(a)).

A starboard tack boat can sail in a straight line beyond the mark perfectly legitimately to put a port tack boat about (IYRU case 17).

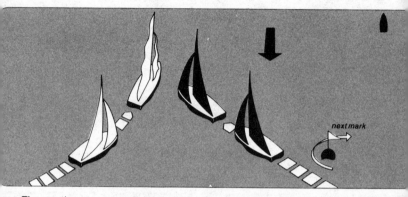

The one time you cannot take the mark away and apply the right-of-way rules to opposite tack boats as in open water is when the starboard tack boat luffs in making the rounding:

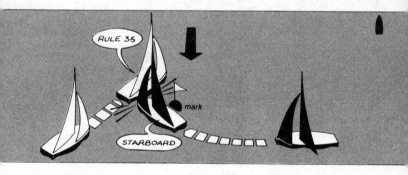

In open water the starboard tack boat would be in the wrong here (except at the start) for altering course when holding right-of-way, in a manner that prevented the other boat keeping clear. When rounding a mark (and at the start) rule 35 specifically allows the right-of-way boat to alter course.

On the same tack – room at the mark

When two boats are overlapped on the same tack the rules apply to room at a mark in the same way as for an offwind mark – rounding (page 51) with only two exceptions (I'll come back to those).

59

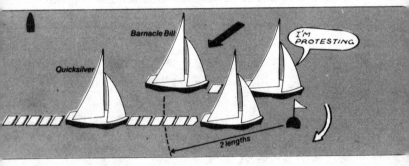

Outside the two lengths circle **Overstander** is required to keep clear as windward boat (rule 37.1), but as soon as the leading boat is 'about to round the mark' the rules that apply to marks come into play and **Overstander** is entitled to room – including room to tack (rule 42.1(a)). 'About to round' is rarely less than two lengths, and could be more.

Barnacle Bill is clear ahead on entering the two lengths circle so at the mark **Quicksilver** has no rights. In the two lengths circle it is irrelevant that **Barnacle Bill** is the windward boat – the rules of mark rounding supersede the windward/ leeward rule here (rules of Section C override earlier rules of Section B with which they conflict).

A leeward boat which has an inside overlap on entering the two lengths circle and is below the lay line is entitled to room to luff round the mark (rule 42.1(a) and 35 (b)(ii)).

The two situations where the overlap rules at the end of a windward leg differ from those at the end of an offwind leg are covered in the two sections immediately following: 'Tacking within the two lengths circle' and 'A special case of room to tack when a mark is big'.

Tacking within the two lengths circle

When either of two boats completes a tack within the two lengths circle the usual water rules don't apply and an overlap can be established and room claimed within two lengths of the mark (**rule 42.3(a)(ii)**).

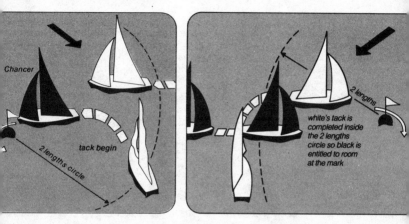

Chancer completes her tack inside the two lengths circle and so is entitled to room at the mark, provided the other boat is able to give it. **Chancer's** tack is still governed by the usual tacking rules so she must not tack in the other boat's water (**rule 41.1,** explained on page 43).

These are the only two situations in which a boat is entitled to claim room after an overlap is gained inside the two lengths circle.

A special case of room to tack when a mark is big

This can only crop up when a mark is big enough to rate as an obstruction (**rule 43.3**).

White must respond to the hail by either:

(a) saying 'I can lay the mark, no water' (or words to that effect) *or*

(b) tacking immediately.

If she tacks, no rules have been broken and there are no grounds for protest. But if she makes the hail and holds on, black must either:

(c) bear away and keep out of white's way *or*

(d) repeat the call for water and take the penalty for an infringement after being given room – which white must give.

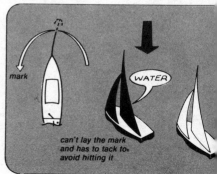

If white calls that she can lay the mark, so that black bears away to keep clear, but white fails to lay it in one, then white is in the wrong.

Tacking at a mark

When two boats approach the mark on opposite tacks and one tacks to round the mark the tacking in water rule (41.1) applies (rule 42.(a)).

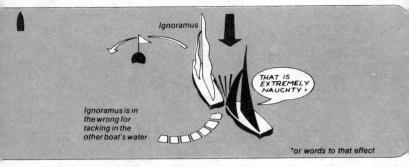

Ignoramus

THAT IS EXTREMELY NAUGHTY *

Ignoramus is in the wrong for tacking in the other boat's water

*or words to that effect

tacking

YOU CAN'T DO THAT

I JUST DID

When both boats approach a mark on the same tack with one clear ahead of the other on entering the two lengths circle, the tacking in water rule (41.1) again applies. The white boat on the left is tacking in the other's water (rule 42.2(c)).

It is important to remember, though, that a tack does not start until the instant the boat passes head to wind. So a luff by the leader which doesn't go beyond head to wind is safe – as in the situation below (rule 42.2(a), definition of tacking and USYRU case 138).

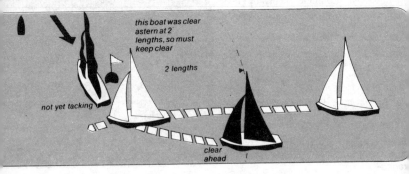

this boat was clear astern at 2 lengths, so must keep clear

2 lengths

not yet tacking

clear ahead

A following boat may not luff higher than close-hauled to prevent the boat ahead tacking (rule 42.2(b) and 35(b)(ii)).

A leading boat which enters the two lengths circle clear ahead may slow down forcing the boat astern onto the outside, then claim room to round once the overlap is made (rule 42.1(a))

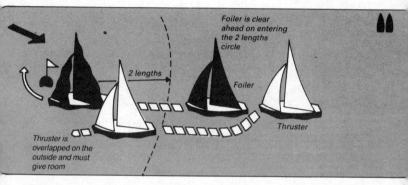

Foiler is clear ahead on entering the 2 lengths circle

2 lengths

Foiler

Thruster

Thruster is overlapped on the outside and must give room

Foiler does nothing wrong here. She is entitled to slow down, and once **Thruster** gets an outside overlap **Foiler** can claim room and, when she's been given it, tack. **Thruster** cannot nudge past **Foiler** to windward, and then call for room at the mark– though that's what two out of three will try.

A special case on a port hand rounding

Both **Complacent** and **Ricochet** must keep clear of **Starboard** under rule 36 while on port tack and under rule 41.1 while tacking. **Ricochet** should have acted sooner when she had the right either to hail **Complacent** for room to tack to keep clear of **Starboard** or to bear away to pass astern of **Starboard**, in which case **Ricochet**, as the outside boat under rule 42.1(a), was required to give **Complacent**, the inside overlapping boat, room to do the same. In the situation shown, **Ricochet** has left it too late to do that. If, in responding to **Ricochet**'s hail, **Complacent** collides with the mark, **Ricochet** will be in the wrong for forcing another boat to infringe a rule.

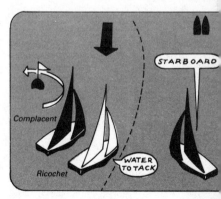

STARBOARD

Complacent

Ricochet

WATER TO TACK

Sailing another boat past a mark

This is a manoeuvre used in team racing and accidentally by beginners in individual racing.

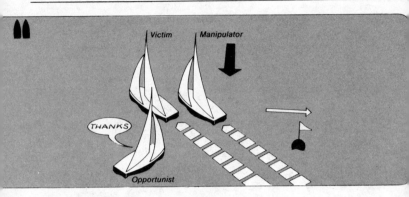

There is no rule to stop **Manipulator** sailing as far beyond the weather mark as she likes, forcing **Victim** to overstand and letting **Opportunist** round ahead (IYRU case 26). This ploy is very common in team racing. **Manipulator** and **Opportunist** would be team mates and **Victim** would be pushed behind **Opportunist**.

OFFWIND LEG

An offwind leg is one that a boat
can sail on one tack.

OPPOSITE TACKS

Port and starboard
Port gives way to starboard (rule 36). This is an important rule.

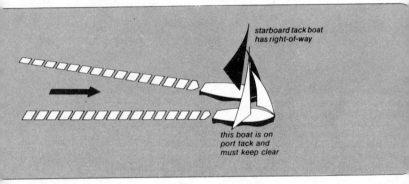

Care is sometimes required in applying this rule. It is important to question how long the relative rights have existed before any collision. If, for example, the starboard boat gybes into a position which gives her right-of-way, she must do so far enough away to allow the port boat to keep clear without her having to begin to alter course until after the gybe has been completed (rules 41.2 and 35).

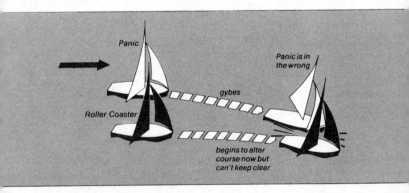

Had **Panic** been on starboard tack all along, and made the alteration of course shown in the diagram, **Roller Coaster** would be in the wrong (rule 36). The starboard-tack boat is allowed to sail any course she likes provided she does not prevent the port-tack boat from keeping clear (rule 35, IYRU case 35).

Overtaking

In open water the port and starboard rule (36) applies when boats on opposite tack are overtaking one another. The rule which says that a boat clear astern keeps clear of a boat ahead (rule 37.2) only applies when both are on the same tack.

The ruling is reversed when the boats are sailing alongside a continuous obstruction. The rule which governs the passing of marks and obstructions when clear ahead and clear astern (rule 42.2) then overrides the port and starboard rule, so the boat clear astern would have to keep clear (IYRU case 68).

Room to pass a continuous obstruction

When two boats are overlapped and sailing alongside a continuous obstruction, the boat ahead must be given room, regardless of what tacks they are on. (Rule 42.1(a) overrides the port and starboard rule (36) here, IYRU case 68.)

The gaining of the overlap by the inside boat is governed by exactly the same rules as when the boats are on the same tack (page 71). So when a port-tack boat is ahead and there is insufficient room for a starboard-tack boat to pass in safety between the boat ahead and the shore, the starboard-tack boat must give room – so she'll have to overtake on the outside!

Room at an obstruction which is not continuous
The same as for 'Offwind Same Tack' (page 72).

▲▲ Starboard tack boat sailing above a proper course

A starboard tack boat may sail any course and the port tack boat is required to keep clear (rule 36, IYRU cases 35 and 17).

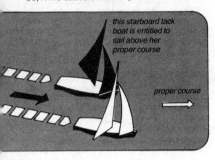

this starboard tack boat is entitled to sail above her proper course

proper course

But the starboard tack boat must establish her rights in sufficient time (as in 'Port and Starboard' above) and not alter course in a way that prevents the other boat from keeping clear (rule 35 and IYRU case 35).

This situation is quite different from the luffing situations described in 'Off-wind Same Tack' (page 72); the boats here are on the opposite tacks so the luffing rules do not apply. If white were to gybe the luffing rules would apply and black (without luffing rights) would be required not to sail above her proper course (rule 38.2(a)).

SAME TACK

▲ Windward boat keeps clear

A windward boat is required to keep clear of a leeward boat (rule 37.1).

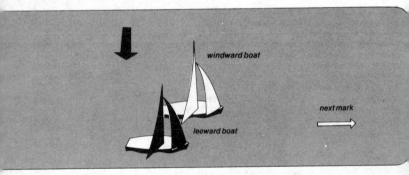

windward boat

next mark

leeward boat

When a leeward boat is sailing her proper course (explained on page 19) and collides with, or has to alter course to avoid, a windward boat the windward boat is in the wrong. The rule is an important one, but in some situations may be overriden, depending on exactly how the two boats approached each other. These overriding situations are dealt with in this section.

▲ Bearing down

A boat within three lengths of another and clear of obstructions must not sail below her proper course when the other boat is steering a course to leeward of the boat ahead, or is overlapped to leeward (rule 39 and USYRU case 127).

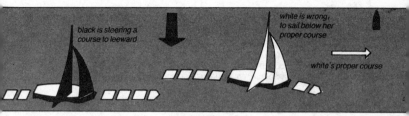

black is steering a course to leeward

white is wrong to sail below her proper course

white's proper course

A protest by black here would be successful, provided she could establish that white was sailing below her (white's) proper course. No collision would be necessary to prove the point. It is normal, though not essential, for the leeward boat to give the boat bearing down a warning shout and only protest if the bearing down continues. White could have this protest dismissed, provided white's course could reasonably have been her proper course.

Overtaking one other boat

One boat clear astern is required to keep clear (rule 37.2).

YOU CAN'T DO THAT

I JUST DID

GO HOME THEN

More often an overtaking boat doesn't follow exactly in the wake of the boat ahead, but to leeward.

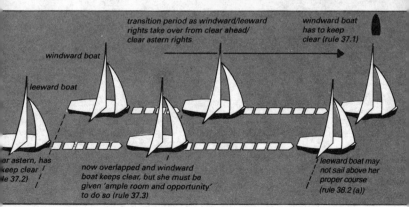

transition period as windward/leeward rights take over from clear ahead/clear astern rights

windward boat has to keep clear (rule 37.1)

windward boat

leeward boat

clear astern, has to keep clear (rule 37.2)

now overlapped and windward boat keeps clear, but she must be given 'ample room and opportunity' to do so (rule 37.3)

leeward boat may not sail above her proper course (rule 38.2 (a))

The obligation to keep clear switches as the overlap is gained. First the boat clear astern has to keep clear, then the windward/leeward rule takes over. As soon as the overlap is established the windward boat is required to begin any necessary avoiding action, but the leeward boat must give her 'ample room and opportunity to keep clear' and must not sail 'above her proper course'. 'Ample room and opportunity' (rule 37.3) means more than just 'sufficient' and the benefit of any doubt must go to the windward boat. Even so, the windward boat may well have to sail above her proper course in fulfilling her obligation to keep clear (IYRU case 25).

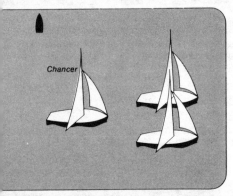

Overtaking more than one boat

A following boat is entitled to sail into an overlapped position between two boats ahead only when there is enough room for her to pass between them (rule 42.3(b) and IYRU cases 27, 67 and 69).

The gap is not big enough for **Chancer** to sail right through so she has no right to push her nose in.

Here the gap is wide enough:

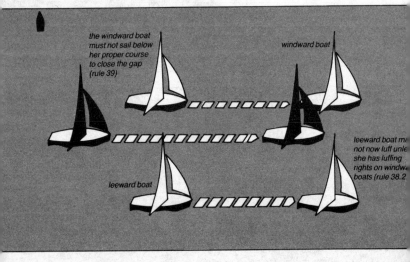

the windward boat must not sail below her proper course to close the gap (rule 39)

windward boat

leeward boat may not now luff unless she has luffing rights on windward boats (rule 38.2)

leeward boat

Black is entitled to sail into the gap because there is enough room for her to sail right through (rule 42.3(b)) (IYRU case 67).

In the following situation the rules apply differently. This time the windward boat is slightly back from the leeward boat, though still overlapped. **Prudence** therefore first overlaps the windward boat, without overlapping the leeward boat.

the gap is now wide enough for Prudence to sail through

windward boat must keep clear of Prudence (rule 37.1)

rudence – not verlapped on e leeward boat

Prudence

leeward boat

The right-of-way between **Prudence** and the windward boat is not now altered by the presence of the leeward boat because **Prudence** does not overlap it. **Prudence** can, therefore, sail her proper course to windward of the boat ahead and the windward boat must widen the gap (her rights before she overlaps the leeward boat are dealt with above in 'Overtaking one other boat').

Room to pass a continuous obstruction

A following boat is only entitled to sail into a gap between a boat ahead and a continuous obstruction, such as a shoreline, when, at the moment the overlap is first established, there is enough room for her to sail safely through the gap (IYRU case 69).

shoreline

this boat was entitled to sail between the other boat and the shore because there was room for her to sail through the gap (rule 42.3 (b))

this boat may not luff, but must give room, since the inside boat gained a legitimate overlap (rule 42.1 (a))

The overtaking boat takes a risk in going for the gap close to the shore unless there is clearly enough room for her to get right through when she first establishes the overlap (IYRU case 69).

Room at an obstruction which is not continuous

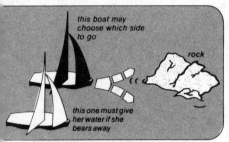

this boat may choose which side to go

rock

this one must give her water if she bears away

The overlap and room-claiming rights here are similar to those for passing a mark (pages 51 – 53), but with the difference that the boats requiring room may choose to go either side of the obstruction and cannot be penalised for touching it.

There is no rule which dictates that a boat should take the shortest route round an obstruction.

Luffing rights – two boat situations

The idea behind the luffing rule is very simple; its application is unfortunately complicated, so be warned.

A helmsman who is being overtaken to windward, or is about to be overtaken to windward, has considerable powers of retaliation under the rules (rule 38). He can luff as high as head to wind without warning and as suddenly as he likes, provided the other boat is:

1. on the same tack and
2. *either* clear astern
   or overlapped upwind and the helmsman of this windward boat has not been at or forward of a 'mast abeam' position since the establishment of the overlap.

The 'mast abeam' position can most simply be explained as follows:

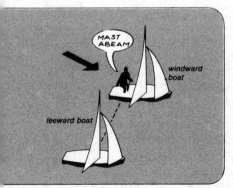

MAST ABEAM

windward boat

leeward boat

The helmsman of the windward boat here is in the 'mast abeam' position because, with the boats sailing parallel (that's important), he can sight the mast of the leeward boat as he looks directly across his own boat from his normal helming position (rule 38.2(a)).

There is no restriction on the sharpness of the leeward boat's luff, except that if serious damage is caused in a collision she will be disqualified as well as the windward boat (rule 32).

The way in which the overlap is established is crucial in deciding whether a leeward boat has luffing rights. There are five ways the leeward boat may gain these rights:

1. When the windward boat establishes an overlap from astern the leeward boat has luffing rights until the windward boat works into a position to have them nullified (as explained in 'Stopping a luff' **page 75**).

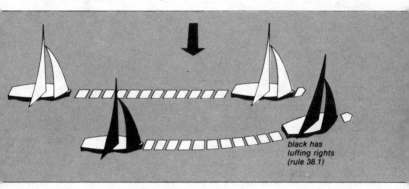

black has luffing rights (rule 38.1)

2. Where two boats are converging and neither is clear astern an overlap, for the purposes of luffing, is considered as beginning when they come within two lengths of the longer boat (rule 38.2(b)).

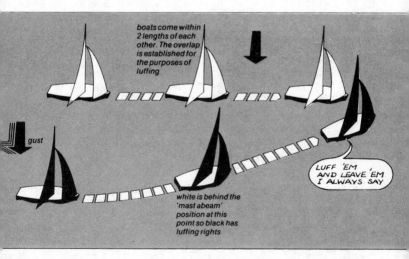

boats come within 2 lengths of each other. The overlap is established for the purposes of luffing

gust

white is behind the 'mast abeam' position at this point so black has luffing rights

LUFF 'EM AND LEAVE 'EM I ALWAYS SAY

3. At the moment of starting, a leeward boat automatically has luffing rights if the windward boat is aft of the 'mast abeam' position (rule 38.2(b)).

4. Luffing rights are also established when either or both boats gybe into a position in which the new windward helmsman is aft of the 'mast abeam' position (rule 38.2(b)).

she gybes

she now has
luffing rights

5. A boat which completes a tack to leeward of another automatically has luffing rights if, at the moment the tack is completed, the windward boat is aft of 'mast abeam' position (rule 38.2(b)).

Luffing rights – more than two boats

Before a leeward boat can luff a bunch of overlapping windward boats she must have luffing rights over all of them if she's to luff legitimately (rule 38.2(e)).

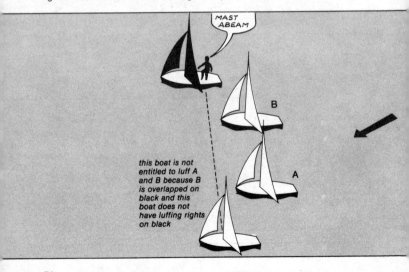

MAST
ABEAM

B

A

this boat is not
entitled to luff A
and B because B
is overlapped on
black and this
boat does not
have luffing rights
on black

Stopping a luff

A leeward helmsman must stop luffing a windward boat when any of the four following cases apply:

- He is given a 'mast abeam' call by the windward helmsman. If he doesn't like the call he can protest, but he must respond to it nevertheless, because the hail itself removes the leeward yacht's luffing rights. For a 'mast abeam' call by the windward helmsman to be valid, the windward boat must have reached a position in relation to the leeward boat so that if they are on parallel courses (or the windward boat is sailing lower) an imaginary line through the windward boat's helmsman (sitting in his normal position), at right angles to the fore-and-aft line of the windward boat, would pass through the mast of the leeward boat. When the windward boat is sailing higher than the leeward boat, the imaginary line is at right angles to the fore-and-aft line of the leeward boat (rule 38.2(a)). The call is important because without it the leeward helmsman can luff so long as there is doubt about whether the 'mast abeam' position has been reached.
- There is no doubt that the 'mast abeam' position has been passed (even if there is no call).
- The windward helmsman hails 'obstruction', or words to that effect, to warn the luffing boat that there is some obstruction to windward.
- The windward helmsman is prevented from responding by an obstruction or a boat over which the luffing boat does not have luffing rights (rule 38.2(d) and 42.1(a)).

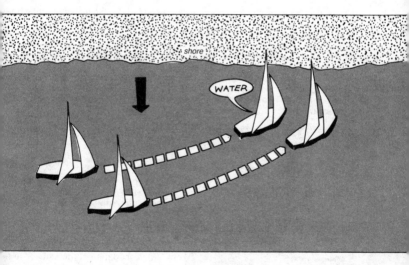

Once a luff has been stopped by the windward boat the leeward boat must bear away to her proper course (rule 38.1 and 38.2(d)) – that is, the proper course from the point at which the luff ends, not the course that was proper before the luff started – even if she has to gybe to do so (IYRU case 63).

The leeward helmsman is required to respond to the hail immediately. If he does and there is a collision – even between his tiller extension and the windward boat – the windward boat is in the wrong. But when the leeward boat has to gybe to take up her proper course the original leeward boat will be in the wrong if the collision happens while she is actually gybing,(RYA case 7 1975). The leeward boat must therefore bear away and gybe quickly to keep out of trouble.

When a leeward helmsman refuses to bear off in response to a legitimate 'mast abeam' hail and the windward helmsman gets upset and collides by bearing away to his proper course, both boats are in the wrong: the leeward boat for not responding to the hail, the windward boat for not keeping clear (USYRU case 15).

Sailing above a proper course without luffing rights

A leeward boat which does not have luffing rights over a windward boat is not entitled to sail above her proper course (rule 38.2(a)).

When the windward boat argues that the leeward boat is sailing above her proper course the onus is on the windward boat to prove her case. The leeward boat must be given the benefit of any doubt (IYRU case 25).

When the leeward boat has to gybe to fulfil her obligation not to sail above her proper course she must gybe (IYRU case 63).

When a leeward boat refuses to go onto her proper course the windward boat would be wise not to bear off and cause a collision – better to keep clear and protest.

GYBING

A boat which is gybing keeps clear

A boat which is gybing is required to keep clear of a boat which isn't (rule 41.1).

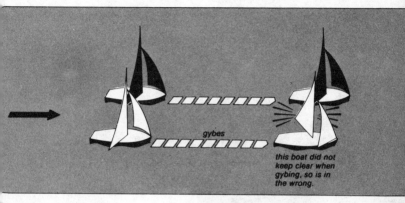

this boat did not
keep clear when
gybing, so is in
the wrong.

Simultaneous gybing

When two boats are both gybing at the same time the one on the other's port side keeps clear (rule 41.4). The easy way to remember simultaneous gybing and tacking onus is quoted in *Elvström Explains* – 'If you're on the right, you're in the right'.

WHO'S WRONG?

both gybe

YOU ARE

THE FINISH

The finish ends racing; it is also the beginning of the protest period – when this book may be useful.

Finishing

A boat finishes when any part of her crew, hull or equipment in normal position crosses the finish line (definition) after fulfilling any penalty obligations under rule 52.2 (that is, re-rounding the finishing mark).

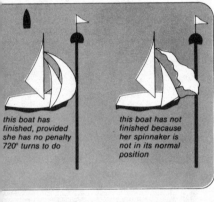

this boat has finished, provided she has no penalty 720° turns to do

this boat has not finished because her spinnaker is not in its normal position

A boat which has finished is still racing until she has cleared the finish line, so a boat which infringes a rule before she has cleared the finish line, but after she has finished, must take her penalty for the infringement.

In the incident below, the port tack boat (white) would not have been penalised if she had been clear of the finish line – that is, no longer intersecting any part of it – since she would not have been racing. Neither boat would then have been penalised (USYRU case 99).

To clear the finish line it is not necessary to sail right across it. The boat below has finished and cleared the line quite legitimately (rule 51.3 and 5).

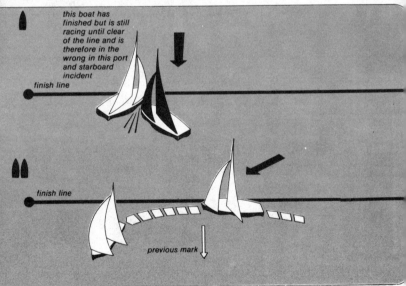

this boat has finished but is still racing until clear of the line and is therefore in the wrong in this port and starboard incident

finish line

finish line

previous mark

A boat also finishes correctly when capsized and the tide carries her across the finish line – provided all the crew are with the boat. But the crew may not swim the capsized boat to the finish line (rule 54).

Hitting a finishing mark

Hitting a finishing mark without having cleared the finish line is exonerated by sailing clear of other boats and doing a 720 degree turn. The finishing position is counted from the moment the first part of the boat, crew or equipment crosses the finish line thereafter.

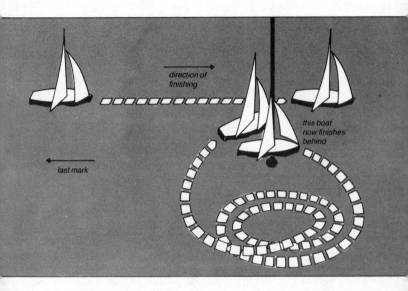

direction of finishing

this boat now finishes behind

last mark

When a boat has crossed and clears the finish line and sailed clear of the marks, but then drifts or sails back and hits a finishing mark she is not penalised for the collision because she is no longer racing (definition). The right-of-way rules apply only to boats which are racing (RYA case 8 1972 and USYRU case 136).

Finish lines

Hook finishes of the kind shown here cannot be enforced by the sailing instructions. Sailing instructions may only override parts of Sections II and III.

They don't override the definition of finishing, which says that a boat finishes when she 'crosses the finish line from the direction of the course from the last mark' which is clearly the opposite direction to that shown in my diagram, since the last mark is taken to be the last turning mark and not a mark used as a finishing mark (IYRU case 102 and USYRU case 84).

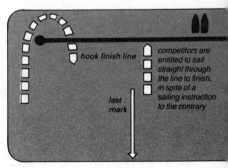

hook finish line

competitors are entitled to sail straight through the line to finish, in spite of a sailing instruction to the contrary

last mark

OTHER IMPORTANT SAILING RULES, ENFORCEMENT AND PENALTIES

Competitive sailors are their own umpires. If we want rules in our racing, every one of us has an interest in taking our penalties when we ourselves break rules and protesting when someone else does. Otherwise, anarchy.

OTHER IMPORTANT SAILING RULES

Rights of a boat anchored

A boat which is anchored has right-of-way over one which is not. However, an anchored boat must let any boats liable to foul her know that she is at anchor. When two boats are anchored close to one another, the one which anchored last keeps clear, except that a boat dragging keeps clear of one that is not (rule 46.4).

Anchoring includes lowering any weight to the bottom, or the crew standing on the bottom holding onto the boat. Anchoring does not mean tying up to or holding onto a mooring, moored boat or jetty. Nor does it mean standing on a jetty to hold the boat (rule 53.3).

Rights of a boat capsized or aground

A capsized or grounded boat is still racing (rule 46.1), but is not penalised for a collision with another boat. Nor is the other boat penalised if the grounding or capsize happens immediately in front of her (rule 46.2). However, a boat aground must tell any boats which might foul her that she is aground. This is one of only three situations where a collision between two boats racing does not necessarily mean that a protest committee has to disqualify someone (rule 46). One is when a boat has just capsized; another is assisting a boat in distress (see below).

Assisting a boat in distress

When in a position to do so, every boat must help any boat or person in peril (fundamental rule A). Note also rule 46.2. A boat may have any disadvantage she suffers in assisting a boat in distress rectified (rule 69 explained on page 90).

The contact rule

This rule (33) was brought in to tighten up rule observance by placing an onus on people to protest after a collision. Paragraph 1 says that when there is contact between the hulls, equipment or crew of two yachts, both shall be disqualified unless one of them retires in acknowledgement of an infringement of the rules or accepts an alternative penalty or one or both of them acts in accordance with rule 68 (Protests by Yachts).

Notice that both boats may be disqualified under this rule for any kind of contact, so when a boom of one boat collides with a sail of the other, both boats would be disqualified under rule 33 on protest if neither had protested or taken an appropriate penalty.

A third boat which protests that two others collided and that neither took their penalties nor flew protest flags is herself required to fly a protest flag. But when the two boats come ashore and no protest is lodged, although a protest flag was flown by one (or both) of them, a third helmsman witnessing the collision may then lodge a protest, even after the normal time limit has expired and if he didn't display a flag (rule 68.3(b)).

When a race committee sees a collision which did not result in a protest or voluntary penalty they may call a protest hearing of both boats involved (rule 70.2(a), (b), (c), (d) and the final paragraph of the rule). The race committee are not *obliged* to act under rule 70 (although they must if a protest is properly lodged on the same incident by a competitor). Even if the collision happened right in front of the race officer they need do nothing, though in that case they would be wise to act.

But if they do decide to act, any protest brought under this rule must be given a formal hearing. The boats cannot be summarily disqualified on the say-so of a witness to the collision, even if he's the race officer.

When contact between two boats is minor and unavoidable the protester may withdraw the protest (rule 68.9).

Fair sailing

The fair sailing rule is designed to catch people who have done something naughty which has somehow not been covered by the complex net of the main rules. It only applies when no other rule can be invoked. So any protest hearing in which the fair sailing rule is used must be long if the case is to be properly considered: the protest committee is required to scour the rule book for any other rule which might apply instead. The rule is the first in the book.

Unfair sailing is one of those terms which cannot be precisely defined, since what is unfair to one sailor may be perfectly fair and all part of the game to another. This rule has tended, recently, to be used to catch out people whose ingenuity has lent itself to novel ways of disqualifying opponents. Intent is important here. A boat was disqualified when her crew deliberately stretched out an arm to hit a windward boat which was keeping clear (RYA case 6 1971). Another was disqualified for deliberately heeling the boat to windward so that the mast would collide with an overtaking windward boat (RYA case 9 1969). (This rule is used extremely rarely.)

Illegal propulsion

The basic principle of the revised rule 54 is set out in the definition of sailing and rule 54.1(a): 'a yacht shall compete only by *sailing*'; sailing is using 'no source of power other than wind and water to increase, maintain or decrease speed.'

In general terms, this means that you can move the crew's bodyweight to trim the boat, but not to impart energy into the boat to drive it forward. You can move the sails to adjust for a change in wind strength or direction, but the move itself must not drive the boat forward.

There are some exceptions: you can propel your boat in any way you like if you are going to help someone in distress, or recovering a person overboard, or rendering assistance. When surfing or planing conditions exist, you may pump (i.e. rapidly trim and release) any sail, or all sails, once, in order to initiate surfing or planing. The full purchase of the mainsheet must be used, so apart from the first direction-changing block on the boat, all blocks must be in use when you pump. This doesn't stop you grabbing all the sheet parts when you gybe because you're not doing it to pump.

You can roll tack, provided that the tacking manoeuvre itself does not advance you in the race, and provided that the mast does not move away from the centreline more than once. This makes the swing to leeward just prior to a tack (favourite with some dinghy classes) illegal because the 'once away from the vertical' will be needed in the second part of the tack.

At well organised regattas, a Jury or protest committee will be on the water and will protest competitors it sees infringing the rule. Most competitors applaud such action, which if taken early in the series inevitably results in suppressing the problem of competitors using 'kinetics' to increase their speed.

PENALTIES AND RULE ENFORCEMENT

▲ Disqualification and retirement

A boat which is found by a protest committee to have infringed a rule or a sailing instruction is disqualified from the race in which the infringement happened. One exception is a boat that retired promptly after the incident, but still protested the other boat: if she lost the protest she would not be disqualified but would be counted as having retired (rule 31.1). Another exception is a boat which protests but also takes a 720 degree penalty (when the option has been provided in the sailing instructions).

Retirement for a rule infringement has to happen promptly after the incident or the retiring boat may be disqualified (Fundamental rule D). Promptly does not mean immediately. A reasonable time is allowed to work out whether to retire, exonerate herself (if permitted), protest or do nothing. Two minutes may be too short a time to reach a decision; five minutes I would say is usually too long.

If the sailing instructions specify one of the alternative penalty systems, special penalties apply to any boat which infringes a rule of Part IV (the right-of-way rules). The two most common alternative penalty systems are the 720 degree turns and the percentage rule.

▲ Alternative penalties (Appendix 3)

The standards of rule observance have fallen in recent years. This is partly attributable to a widespread feeling, expressed by a refusal to retire after infringing a rule or to protest against other wrong-doers, that retirement from a race is too harsh a penalty for breaking a rule. The alternative penalty systems were introduced to make it easier for people to acknowledge their errors by paying a lesser price. And generally the systems work well. The 720 degree penalty works best for one design boats, especially the smaller ones, and is explained below. The percentage penalties work best for offshore racing and larger boats. The special appendix that deals with percentage penalties is self explanatory.

Alternative penalties apply only to infringements of rules in Part IV (the right-of-way rules), and use of either system must be specified in the sailing instructions, otherwise retirement and disqualification are in force (rule 3.2(b)(xxii)).

▲ 720 degree turns (Appendix 3)

A boat which breaks a rule of Part IV may exonerate herself by making two full 360 degree turns. She may then carry on with the race.

If she does not acknowledge her error, she may be disqualified after a protest (under rule 68) by another boat or by the race committee (rule 73.2) (Appendix 3, clause 1.5).

The boat which is fouled has to hail the wrongdoer that she intends to protest. The wrongdoer must do her turns at the first reasonable opportunity (clause 1.1). This usually means as soon as she can work into a clear enough patch of water to gyrate without colliding with other boats, and that may sometimes be on the following leg (clause 1.1 does not say 'same leg'). Clear water must be actively sought; it is not good enough to sail on for five minutes waiting for a space to appear (IYRU case 105).

The turns must both be done in the same direction, one immediately after the other, and must be full turns. That means that on windward leg a helmsman may not go into his turns from close-hauled starboard and leave them close-hauled on port as often happens (clause 1.1).

Before the starting signal, the infringing boat must do her turns as soon as she can. If the turns are not properly done, the infringing boat may be disqualified after a properly lodged protest (rule 68 or 70).

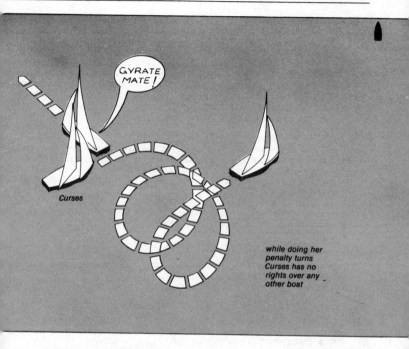

When serious damage is caused in a collision the boat in the wrong may be disqualified, even though she may have done her turns properly (clause 1.4).

It is possible under the 720 degree rule for a helmsman very occasionally to deliberately infringe a rule, do the turns and end up better off after the incident than he would have by obeying the rules. A port tack boat beating to a windward mark, for example, against a strong tide in light air might lose less ground by refusing to give way to a starboard boat and take the penalty turns after rounding the mark than by tacking for the starboard boat and failing to lay the mark.

The port boat then could be disqualified on protest (Appendix 3, clause 1.4 and rules 68 or 70), even though she might have done her turns immediately after the incident.

After a collision and when the turns aren't properly carried out – either through some technicality or only one turn being done – the right-of-way boat is protected by clause 1.5 of Appendix 3 from being disqualified under rule 33 (Contact between yachts, explained on page 84).

Penalty points in team racing

Appendix 4 now includes the 'green flag penalty system'. A helmsman who infringes a rule and acknowledges his infringement continues racing and takes a 2.5 point penalty. If he infringes a second or third time in that race, he takes another 2.5 point penalty for each infringement he acknowledges. A lost protest costs him 6 points.

An acknowledged infringement is signalled by tying a green flag to the shroud and protest is signalled by tying on a red flag. Once a helmsman flies a green flag he may no take it down and fly a red one to protest over the incident. But if he first puts up a red on with the intention of protesting, then thinks better of it, he may take it down and fly th green one – provided the switch happens promptly after the incident.

The advantage of this system is that the balance of a team race is not destroye either by losing a boat from one team or by the excessive points penalty of a well-place boat being disqualified. Its provisions must be stated clearly in the sailing instruction The 720 degree penalty has also been found to work well in team races.

The penalty for not protesting

After a collision with another boat, failure to protest may mean disqualification. If the other boa doesn't protest, either a third boat or anyone else who saw the incident may have both boat disqualified after a protest hearing (rule 33, explained on page 84).

When a rule infringement does not result in a collision there is little risk of disqualificatio in failing to lodge a protest.

A boat which hits a mark must either retire (or do a 720 penalty turn) or protest – even she was forced onto the mark – although when the boat that forced her onto the mark takes th penalty for the infringement, no protest is necessary (rule 52.1).

Making the rules work

Except in match races (just two boats), there can be no effective umpires or referees in sailin as there are in games like football and cricket. With sometimes over a hundred competitors bi no ball to blaze a trail of fouls, the practical difficulties of even seeing fouls on the water ai enormous. To make matters worse, the complexity of the sailing rules would make any instar decisions by an untrained referee extremely unreliable. We sailors are therefore our ow umpires. When people foul us and don't take their voluntary penalty we should protest; whe we break a rule we should take our penalty voluntarily.

In a fleet where nobody ever protests or retires, the rules cease to exist. The racing i then decidedly less satisfactory than when behaviour on the water is controlled – at leas approximately – by a known code, the IYRU rules.

Protest by one competitor against another

When a helmsman thinks he has been fouled by another boat – whether there is a collision not – or when he thinks any other competitor has broken a rule or infringed one of the sailin instructions, he is entitled to protest (rule 68.1). A protest is decided ashore by a protest con mittee, which is usually a sub-committee of the race committee. It acts in much the same wa as a court of law, first hearing the evidence and then giving its verdict as to which boats, if an are disqualified.

A helmsman who decides to protest must fly a protest flag (rule 68.2). Code flag B is alway acceptable, but any flag will usually do. In one case a piece of red cellophane was allowe (USYRU case 88).

A protest flag must be flown in the rigging, except in a singlehander where it m be waved by the protesting helmsman soon after the incident and waved again finishing.

A protest committee is only allowed to hear a protest for which no flag was flov when:

1. The facts of the incident were not known until after the finish – for example, wher boat is alleged to have touched another and her crew was unaware of any collision the time. But ignorance of a rule interpretation or a sailing instruction does not rate

a reason for failing to fly a protest flag at the time of an incident (rule 68.4, IYRU case 47).
. Seeking redress about some action or omission of the race committee (rule 69).
. The boat protesting is dismasted (USYRU case 153), capsized or sunk.
. A boat sees a collision between two others and neither of the colliding boats goes through with a protest, although one or both flew flags soon after the incident (rules 33 and 68.4).

Otherwise, a protest flag must be flown 'at the first reasonable opportunity' after the incident rule 68.3(b)). This is vague, but appeal cases have made the intention fairly clear: the flag must be flown within 'a reasonably short time' of the incident (USYRU case 3). When a clear statement of the intention to protest is made at the time of the incident, more latitude may be allowed in putting up the flag – although allowing as legitimate a flag which first appeared two miles after the incident (USYRU case 105) is a unique case and should not be quoted as a precedent. In extremely heavy weather, the 'first reasonable opportunity' in a boat which relies primarily for crew weight on stability may well be after the finish.

'A protesting yacht shall try to inform the yacht protested against that a protest will be lodged' (rule 68.2). The attempt is the important thing. The helmsman protested against need not necessarily have heard the call. Unless an alternative penalty system is in force (when the hail must be immediate) there is no time limit on when the attempt should be made.

On coming ashore the boat protesting must put in a written protest to the race committee (rule 68.5 and IYRU case 29). The protest must be delivered within two hours of the time the protester finishes, although when a race committee feel that particular circumstances justify them in extending the time limit they may do so (rule 68.6). Sailing instructions often set different time limits which override the standard IYRU ruling.

The defendant is entitled to see and study the protest. If he asks for it and is not given it, the protest would be dismissed on appeal (USYRU case 82). If he doesn't ask for it, that would not be grounds on which an appeal would be dismissed (USYRU case 133).

The practice of charging a protest fee returnable only to the helmsman who is not disqualified is decidedly not recommended; it discourages protests, which in turn encourages greater rule abuse. If race committees fine well-meaning people for losing protests, who is ever going to protest? And without protests there is no such thing as rule observance.

Protest by a race committee

A race committee can call on its own initiative for a protest hearing to deal with a possible rule infringement by a competitor (rule 70.2). The hearing is carried out as though a protest has been made against the infringing boat by another competitor (rule 70.2(d) and (e)).

A race committee can start its own proceedings in the following circumstances:
. A member of the race committee may have seen the infringement.
. The infringement is reported the same day by a disinterested non-competitor.
. The race committee may have grounds for believing that an infringement resulted in serious damage.
. A boat in a protest may have committed some other infringement (rule 70.2).
. The race committee may have learned from a written or oral statement from a boat that she may have infringed a rule. A 'written statement' includes an invalid protest form (rule 70.2(b)).

But, except for an alleged infringement of rule 54 (Means of Propulsion), however blatant a competitor's infringement, the race committee is not allowed to disqualify any boat without a formal hearing, provided that the boat started and finished correctly (rule 70.1(a) and the last sentence of 70.2).

▲ **Disqualification without a hearing**

The only infringements for which a race committee may disqualify a boat without a hearing ar failing to start or finish correctly, or for infringing rule 54 (Means of Propulsion). Even then, competitor who is disqualified without a hearing is entitled to one if he simply asks the rac committee (rule 70.1(c)).

▲ **Seeking redress from the race committee**

This is difficult to win, partly because the protest committee, being a sub-committee the race committee, is often inclined to regard the point of view of a hard-worked rac officer more sympathetically than a trouble-making, self-interested competitor. A goc protest committee will guard against this tendency and weigh the evidence as fairly a possible.

The request is not strictly against the race committee, but is a plea by a helmsma that his finishing position has been 'materially prejudiced . . .by an action or omission the race committee' (rule 69). The protest committee must proceed in accordance wi rule 74.2. From 74.2(c), the arrangements which the race committee may make incluc the following:

The protest committee must proceed in accordance with rule 74.2. From 74.2 (c), th arrangements which the race committee may make include the following:

(i) to let the results of the race stand; or

(ii) to award the prejudiced yacht points according to her recorded position at th rounding mark before the incident; or

(iii) when the incident occurs close enough to the finishing line to enable the rac committee to determine the prejudiced yacht's probable finishing position, award her the points she would have scored if she had finished in that positio or

(iv) to award the prejudiced yacht breakdown points when rule 69 (c) applies; or

(v) to award the prejudiced yacht points in accordance with Appendix 5 – Olymp Scoring System, para. 3; or

(vi) in a single race for prizes, assuming that the prejudiced yacht qualifies for on to award her an additional prize to her; or

(vii) to *abandon* or *cancel* the race; or

(viii) to adopt any other means,

provided that the race committee's arrangement is as equitable as possible to all th yachts concerned.

The rule also covers giving assistance to someone in distress while racing, and bein disabled by a boat that is in the wrong. Any doubt about the anticipated finishing positic of the boat giving assistance, or disabled, should be resolved in favour of that boat.

A race abandoned or cancelled is unfair to the people who were up front that day, there is a different solution which is reasonably fair to everybody, that's the one th committee should go for. If not, the race must be abandoned.

When there is reasonable doubt about whether a competitor was prejudiced, th doubt must be resolved in favour of the competitor (USYRU case 66).

Composition of a protest committee

A protest committee is appointed by the race committee and is, strictly, part of the race committee. No-one may be on a protest committee who might benefit from that committee's decision. Interpreted strictly, this would bar competitors from protest committees (USYRU case 124), but in practice competitors can be included provided both protester and defendant agree to it. So at the start of the hearing, the protester and defendant should be asked whether they object to any member of the protest committee, those members who competed in the race or the series being pointed out. If there are no objections, any right of appeal on that score is automatically invalid (USYRU case 175).

Extra care in the appointment of a protest committee is called for when a competitor seeks redress from the race committee for some error or oversight in the running of a race (rule 69). The race committee is then sitting in judgement on itself through its protest committee. Ideally the protest committee should consist of people who were neither involved in the race as competitors nor as organisers. Then injustice is not seen to be done.

The right to appeal

The final arbiter in a dispute over the IYRU rules is the national sailing authority of the country in which the event is sailed. However, a formal appeal to the national authority can only be considered on questions of rule interpretation, not on questions of fact. the final arbiter of fact is the protest committee (rule 74.1).

For some major events like World Championships, a special jury is appointed which is competent enough for there to be no right of appeal. This waiving of appeal is also common in two day team racing events where teams must be eliminated from early rounds before there can be a final and winners. An appeal on a first round result would dislocate the whole event.

The right to waive appeal is only given by a national or the international sailing authority; it is not given lightly.

Counter-protest

It often happens that both boats involved in an incident lodge a protest. If both protests are valid, they may be heard simultaneously. The onus of proof will in no way change. However, if one boat in a collision fails to protest, or fails to fly a protest flag properly, and the other boat does not lodge a valid protest, neither boat may have her protest heard (USYRU case 49).

The protest hearing

The procedure for hearing a protest is well explained in Appendix 6 of the IYRU rules. It is important to follow this carefully, because a hearing in which there are major errors of procedure may invalidate a protest (USYRU case 54). But if either the protester or defendant (referred to as 'protestee' in the rule book) feels that procedural errors are being made, these should be pointed out at the time. Failure to complain at the time, or as soon afterwards as the wrong procedure became known, would mean that an appeal based on the procedural errors would be dismissed (USYRU case 176).

The defendant and the protester have the right to be present at the hearing and throughout the taking of evidence (rule 73.1). When either the defendant or protester has made a reasonable attempt to be present he should be allowed to be present. So if a committee has several protests to hear, it should hear those where both parties are present first (USYRU case 104). But if an interested party fails to make an effort to be at the hearing, a committee may deal with the case without a full hearing (rule 73.5 and USYRU case 54).

The protester and defendant may call as many witnesses as they choose (rule 73.1) unless witnesses re-iterate facts that have already been established (USYRU case 54).

A protest committee should put its findings in writing in the form 'facts found: . . .' and 'decisions: . . .' quoting the rule numbers that apply. There is no obligation to do it this way though, unless asked to do so (USYRU case 54). Otherwise it may give its decision orally (rule 74.7).

Appeals

A party to a protest may appeal against a decision of a protest committee solely on a question of its interpretation of the rules, and a race or protest committee may refer its own decision for confirmation or correction of its interpretation of the rules.

The appeal or reference must comply with the requirements of rule 78, and any prescriptions which a National Authority may have attached to rule 78.

THE 1989-92 INTERNATIONAL YACHT RACING RULES

Introduction

Translation and Interpretation

In translating and interpreting these rules, it shall be understood that the word "shall" is mandatory, and the words "can" and "may" are permissive.

Notes: (a) These rules become effective on May 1, 1989.

(b) Marginal markings indicate the changes made in the 1985 Racing Rules.

(c) No changes are contemplated before 1993.

(d) These rules supersede all previous editions.

CONTENTS

Part IV—RIGHT OF WAY RULES

Part V—OTHER SAILING RULES

Part I—Status of the Rules, Fundamental Rules and Definitions

Status of the Rules

The International Yacht Racing Rules have been established by the International Yacht Racing Union for the organisation, conduct and judging of the sport of yacht racing, and are amended and published every four years by the IYRU in accordance with its Constitution.

A national authority may alter or add to these rules by prescription, with the exception of the rules of Parts I and IV, the definitions of Part VI, rules 1, 3, 26 and 61, and Appendix 14, unless permitted in a rule itself.

The sailing instructions may alter rules only in accordance with rule 3.1, Sailing Instructions.

Fundamental Rules

A. Rendering Assistance

Every yacht shall render all possible assistance to any vessel or person in peril, when in a position to do so.

B. Responsibility of a Yacht

It shall be the sole responsibility of each yacht to decide whether or not to *start* or to continue to *race*.

C. Fair Sailing

A yacht, her owner and crew shall compete only by *sailing*, using their speed and skill, and, except in team racing, by individual effort, in compliance with the **rules** and in accordance with recognised principles of fair play and sportsmanship. A yacht may be penalised under this rule only in the case of a clear-cut violation of the above principles and only when no other **rule** applies, except rule 75, Gross Infringement of Rules or Misconduct.

D. Accepting Penalties

A yacht that realises she has infringed a **rule** shall either retire promptly or accept an alternative penalty when so prescribed in the sailing instructions.

Definitions

When a term defined in Part I is used in its defined sense it is printed in **italic** *type. All preambles and definitions rank as rules. Further definitions will be found at the beginning of Part VI.*

Sailing - A yacht is *sailing* when using only the wind and water to increase, maintain or decrease her speed, with her crew adjusting the trim of sails and hull and performing other acts of seamanship.

Racing - A yacht is *racing* from her preparatory signal until she has either *finished* and cleared the finishing line and finishing *marks* or retired, or until the race has been *postponed, abandoned, cancelled,* or a general recall has been signalled.

Starting - A yacht *starts* when, after fulfilling her penalty obligations, if any, under rule 51.1(c), Sailing the Course, and after her starting signal, any part of her hull, crew or equipment first crosses the starting line in the direction of the course to the first *mark.*

Finishing - A yacht *finishes* when any part of her hull, or of her crew or equipment in normal position, crosses the finishing line in the direction of the course from the last *mark,* after fulfilling her penalty obligations, if any, under rule 52.2(b), Touching a Mark.

Luffing - Altering course towards the wind.

Tacking - A yacht is *tacking* from the moment she is beyond head to wind until she has *borne away* to a *close-hauled* course.

Bearing away - Altering course away from the wind until a yacht begins to *gybe.*

Gybing - A yacht begins to *gybe* at the moment when, with the wind aft, the foot of her mainsail crosses her centre line, and completes the *gybe* when the mainsail has filled on the other *tack.*

On a tack - A yacht is *on a tack* except when she is *tacking* or *gybing.* A yacht is on the *tack (starboard* or *port)* corresponding to her *windward* side.

Close-hauled - A yacht is *close-hauled* when *sailing* by the wind as close as she can lie with advantage in working to windward.

Clear Astern and *Clear Ahead; Overlap* - A yacht is *clear astern* of another when her hull and equipment in normal position are abaft an imaginary line projected abeam from the aftermost point of the other's hull and equipment in normal position. The other yacht is *clear ahead.*

The yachts *overlap* when neither is *clear astern;* or when, although one is *clear astern,* an intervening yacht *overlaps* both of them.

The terms *clear astern, clear ahead* and *overlap* apply to yachts on opposite *tacks* only when they are subject to rule 42, Rounding or Passing Marks and Obstructions.

Leeward and Windward - The *leeward* side of a yacht is that on which she is, or, when head to wind, was, carrying her mainsail. The opposite side is the *windward* side.

When neither of two yachts on the same *tack* is *clear astern*, the one on the *leeward* side of the other is the *leeward yacht*. The other is the *windward yacht*.

Proper Course - A *proper course* is any course that a yacht might *sail* after the starting signal, in the absence of the other yacht or yachts affected, to *finish* as quickly as possible. The course *sailed* before *luffing* or *bearing away* is presumably, but not necessarily, that yacht's *proper course*. There is no *proper course* before the starting signal.

Mark - A *mark* is any object specified in the sailing instructions that a yacht must round or pass on a required side.

Every ordinary part of a *mark* ranks as part of it, including a flag, flagpole, boom or hoisted boat, but excluding ground tackle and any object either accidentally or temporarily attached to the *mark*.

Obstruction - An *obstruction* is any object, including a vessel under way, large enough to require a yacht, when more than one overall length away from it, to make a substantial alteration of course to pass on one side or the other, or any object that can be passed on one side only, including a buoy when the yacht in question cannot safely pass between it and the shoal or object that it marks. The sailing instructions may prescribe that certain defined areas shall rank as *obstructions*.

Postponement - A *postponed* race is one that is not started at its scheduled time and that can be sailed at any time the race committee may decide.

Abandonment - An *abandoned* race is one that the race committee declares void at any time after the starting signal, and that can be re-sailed at its discretion.

Cancellation - A *cancelled* race is one that the race committee decides will not be sailed thereafter.

Part II—Organisation and Management

1 Organising, Conducting and Judging Races

1.1 GOVERNING RULES
The organising authority, race committee, protest committee and all other bodies and persons concerned with the organisation, conduct and judging of a race, regatta or series shall be governed by these rules, the prescriptions of the national authority when they apply, the class rules (except when they conflict with these rules), the sailing instructions and any other conditions governing the event. Hereinafter the term 'race' shall, when appropriate, include a regatta or a series of races.

1.2 ORGANISING AUTHORITY
Races shall be organised by:

(a)   the IYRU; or

(b)   a member national authority of the IYRU; or

(c)   a club or regatta committee affiliated to a national authority; or

(d)   a class association either with the approval of a national authority or in conjunction with an affiliated club or regatta committee; or

(e)   an unaffiliated body in conjunction with an affiliated club or regatta committee;

which will hereinafter be referred to as the organising authority.

The organising authority shall appoint a race committee and publish a notice of race in accordance with rule 2, Notice of Race.

1.3 RACE COMMITTEE
The race committee shall publish sailing instructions in accordance with rule 3, Sailing Instructions, and conduct the race, subject to such direction as the organising authority may exercise. The term "race committee" whenever it is used shall include any person or committee that is responsible for performing any of the duties or functions of the race committee.

1.4 PROTEST COMMITTEES
The receiving, hearing, and deciding of protests and other matters arising under the rules of Part VI, Protests, Penalties and Appeals, shall be carried out by:

(a)   the race committee itself; or

(b)   a sub-committee thereof appointed by the race committee and consisting of its own members, or others, or a combination of both; or

(c)   a jury or a protest committee, separate from and independent of the race committee, appointed by the organising authority or the race committee; or

(d)   an international jury appointed by the organising authority in accordance with Appendix 8, International Juries. A national authority may prescribe that its approval is required for the appointment of international juries for events within its jurisdiction other than those of the IYRU.

A jury or protest committee shall not supervise the conduct of the race, or direct the race committee, except when so directed by the organising authority. (The term "jury", as used in yacht racing, means a panel of judges.)

1.5   RIGHT OF APPEAL
Decisions of a **protest committee** may be appealed in accordance with rule 77.1, Right of Appeal, except that:

(a)   there shall be no appeal from the decisions of an international jury constituted in accordance with Appendix 8, International Juries.

(b)   when the notice of race and the sailing instructions so state, the right of appeal may be denied when:

(i)   it is essential to determine promptly the result of a race that will qualify a yacht to compete in a later stage of the event or a subsequent event (a national authority may prescribe that its approval is required for such a procedure); or

(ii)   a national authority so prescribes for a particular event open only to entrants under its own jurisdiction.

1.6   EXCLUSION OF YACHTS AND COMPETITORS
Unless otherwise prescribed by the national authority, the organising authority or the race committee may, before the start of the first race, reject or rescind the entry of any yacht or exclude a competitor, without stating the reason. However, at all world and continental championships, no entry within established quotas shall be rejected or rescinded without first obtaining the approval of the IYRU, the relevant international class association or the Offshore Racing Council.

2   **Notice of Race**

The notice of race shall contain the following information:

(a)   The title, place and dates of the event and name of the organising authority.

(b) That the race will be governed by the International Yacht Racing Rules, the prescriptions of the national authority when they apply (for international events, a copy in English of prescriptions that apply shall be available to each yacht), the rules of each class concerned, and such other rules as are applicable. When class rules are altered, the alterations shall be stated.

(c) The class(es) to *race*, conditions of eligibility or entry and, when appropriate, restrictions on numbers of entries.

(d) The times of registration and starts of the practice race or first race, and succeeding races when known.

The notice shall, when appropriate, include the following:

(e) The category of the event in accordance with Appendix 14, Event Classification and Advertising, and, when required, the additional information prescribed in Appendix 14.

(f) The scoring system.

(g) The time and place at which the sailing instructions will be available.

(h) Variations from the racing rules, subject to rule 3.1, Sailing Instructions.

(i) The procedure for advance registration or entry, including closing dates when applicable, fees and the mailing address.

(j) Measurement procedures or requirements for measuring or rating certificates.

(k) The course(s) to be *sailed*.

(l) Alternative penalties for rule infringements.

(m) Prizes.

(n) Denial of the right of appeal, subject to rule 1.5, Right of Appeal.

3   Sailing Instructions

3.1   STATUS

(a) These rules shall be supplemented by written sailing instructions that shall rank as rules and may, subject to the restrictions of rule 3.1(b), alter a rule by specific reference to it.

(b) Except in accordance with rule 3.2(b) (xxix), the sailing instructions shall not alter:

    (i)   Parts I and IV,

    (ii)   rules 1, 2, 3, 26, 51.1(a) and 61,

    (iii)   the definitions and Sections C and D of Part VI,

    (iv)   Appendix 14, and

(c)   When so prescribed by the national authority, these restrictions shall not preclude the right of developing and testing proposed rule changes in local races. A national authority may also prescribe that its approval is required for such changes.

.2   CONTENTS

(a)   The sailing instructions shall contain the following information:

(i)   That the race will be governed by the International Yacht Racing Rules, the prescriptions of the national authority when they apply (for international events, a copy in English of prescriptions that apply shall be included in the sailing instructions), the rules of each class concerned, the sailing instructions and such other rules as are applicable.

(ii)   The schedule of races, the classes to *race*, and the order and times of warning signals.

(iii) The course to be *sailed* or a list of *marks* from which the course will be selected, describing the *marks*, stating their order and, for each, whether it is to be rounded or passed and on which side.

A diagram or chart is recommended.

(iv)   Description of the starting line, the starting system and any special signals to be used.

(v)   The procedure for individual and general recalls and any special signals.

(vi)   Description of the finishing line and any special instructions for *finishing* a course shortened after the start.

(vii) The time limit, if any, for *finishing*.

(viii) The scoring system, when not previously announced in writing, including the method, if any, for breaking ties.

(b)   The sailing instructions shall, when appropriate, include the following:

(i)   The category of the event in accordance with Appendix 14, Event Classification and Advertising, and, when required, the additional information prescribed in Appendix 14.

(ii)   Variations from the racing rules, subject to rule 3.1, or the class rules for a special race.

(iii) The registration procedure.

(iv)	Location(s) of official notice board(s).
(v)	Procedure for changes in the sailing instructions.
(vi)	Restrictions controlling alterations to yachts when supplied by the organising authority.
(vii)	Signals to be made ashore and location of signal station(s).
(viii)	Class flags.
(ix)	The racing area. A chart is recommended.
(x)	The starting area.
(xi)	Course signals.
(xii)	Approximate course length; approximate length of windward legs.
(xiii)	Information on tides and currents.
(xiv)	Procedure for shortening the course before or after the start.
(xv)	Mark boats; lead boats.
(xvi)	Procedure for changes of course after the start and related signals.
(xvii)	The time limit, if any, for yachts other than the first yacht to *finish*.
(xviii)	Whether races *postponed* or *abandoned* for the day will be sailed later and, if so, when and where.
(xix)	The number of races required to complete the regatta.
(xx)	Safety, such as requirements and signals for personal buoyancy, check-in at the starting area, and check-out and check-in ashore.
(xxi)	Any measurement or inspection procedure.
(xxii)	Alternative penalties for rule infringements.
(xxiii)	Whether declarations are required.
(xxiv)	Protest procedure and times and place of hearings.
(xxv)	Restrictions on use of support boats, plastic pools, radios, etc. and limitations on hauling out.
(xxvi)	Substitute competitors.
(xxvii)	Prizes.
(xxviii)	Time allowances.
(xxix)	Racing rules applicable between sunset and sunrise and night signals to be used by the race committee.

(xxx) Disposition to be made of a yacht appearing at the start alone in her class.

(xxxi) Denial of the right of appeal, subject to rule 1.5, Right of Appeal.

(xxxii) Other commitments of the race committee and obligations of yachts.

3.3 DISTRIBUTION

The sailing instructions shall be available to each yacht entitled to *race*.

3.4 CHANGES

Changes in sailing instructions shall be made in writing before a race by:

(a) posting in proper time on the official notice board, or

(b) being communicated to each yacht on the water before the warning signal, except that oral instructions may be given only on the water in accordance with procedure prescribed in the sailing instructions.

4 Signals

4.1 VISUAL SIGNALS

Unless otherwise prescribed in the sailing instructions, the following International Code flags (or boards) and other visual signals shall be used as indicated, and when displayed alone shall apply to all classes, and when displayed over a class flag shall apply to the designated class only:

"AP", Answering Pendant - Postponement Signal

Means:

(a) "All races not started are *postponed*. The warning signal will be made one minute after this signal is lowered."
(One sound signal shall be made with the lowering of the "AP".)

(b) Over one ball or shape.
"The scheduled starting times of all races not started are *postponed* fifteen minutes."
(This *postponement* can be extended indefinitely by the addition of one ball or shape for every fifteen minutes.)

(c) Over one of the numeral pendants 1 to 9.
"All races not started are *postponed* one hour, two hours, etc."

(d) Over Code flag "A".
"All races not started are *postponed* to a later day."

"B" — Protest signal.

When displayed by a yacht, means:
"I intend to lodge a **protest**."

"C" — Change of Course while Racing.

When displayed at or near a rounding *mark*, means:
"After rounding this *mark*, the course to the next *mark* has been changed."

"I" — Round the Ends Starting Rule

When displayed before or with the preparatory signal, means:
"Rule 51.1(c) will be in effect for this start."

When lowered, accompanied by one long sound signal, one minute before the starting signal, means:
"The one-minute period of rule 51.1(c) has begun."

"L" — Means:

(a) When displayed ashore:
"A notice to competitors has been posted on the official notice board."

(b) When displayed afloat:
"Come within hail", or "Follow me".

"M" — Mark Signal.

When displayed on a buoy, vessel, or other object, means:
"Round or pass the object displaying this signal instead of the *mark* that it replaces."

"N" — Abandonment Signal.

Means:
"All races are *abandoned*."

"N over X" —Abandonment and Re-sail Signal.

Means:
"All races are *abandoned* and will shortly be re-sailed. The warning signal will be made one minute after this signal is lowered."
(One sound signal shall be made with the lowering of "N over X".)

"N over First Substitute" —Cancellation Signal.

Means:
"All races are *cancelled*."

"P" — Preparatory Signal.

Means:
"The class designated by the warning signal will *start* in five minutes exactly."

"S" — Shorten Course Signal.

Means:
(a) at the starting line:
"*Sail* the shortened course as prescribed in the sailing instructions."

(b) at the finishing line:
"*Finish* the race either:
(i) at the prescribed finishing line at the end of the round still to be completed by the leading yacht, or
(ii) as prescribed in the sailing instructions."

(c) at a rounding *mark:*
"*Finish* between the rounding *mark* and the committee boat."

"X" — Individual Recall.

When displayed promptly after the starting signal, accompanied by one sound signal, means:
"One or more yachts are recalled in accordance with rule 8.1, Individual Recall."

"Y" — Life Jacket Signal.
Means:
"Life jackets or other adequate personal buoyancy shall be worn while *racing* by all competitors, unless specifically excepted in the sailing instructions."
When this signal is displayed after the warning signal, failure to comply shall not be cause for disqualification.
Notwithstanding anything in this rule, it shall be the individual responsibility of each competitor to wear a life jacket or other adequate personal buoyancy when conditions warrant. A wet suit is not adequate personal buoyancy.

"First Substitute" —General Recall Signal.

Means:
"The class is recalled for a new start. The preparatory signal will be made one minute after this signal is lowered."
(One sound signal shall be made with the lowering of "First Substitute".)

Red Flag

When displayed by a committee boat, means:
"Leave all *marks* to port."

Green Flag

When displayed by a committee boat, means:
"Leave all *marks* to starboard."

Blue Flag or Shape - Finishing Signal.

When displayed by a committee boat, means:
"The committee boat is on station at the finishing line."

4.2   SPECIAL SIGNALS
The sailing instructions shall designate any other special signals and shall explain their meaning.

4.3   CALLING ATTENTION TO VISUAL SIGNALS
Whenever the race committee makes a signal, except "S" before the warning signal or a blue flag or shape when on station at the finishing line, it shall call attention to its action as follows:

(a)   Three guns or other sound signals when displaying:

   (i)   "N";

   (ii)   "N over X";

   (iii)   "N over First Substitute".

(b)   Two guns or other sound signals when displaying:

   (i)   "AP";

   (ii)   "S";

   (iii)   "First Substitute".

(c)   Repetitive sound signals while displaying Code flag "C".

(d)   One gun or other sound signal when making any other signal, including the lowering of:

   (i)   "AP" when the length of the *postponement* is not signalled;

   (ii)   "N over X";

   (iii)   "First Substitute".

4.4   SIGNALS FOR STARTING A RACE

(a)   Unless otherwise prescribed in the sailing instructions, the signals for starting a race shall be made at five-minute intervals exactly, and shall be either:

System 1	Warning Signal	—	Class flag broken out or distinctive signal displayed.
	Preparatory Signal	—	Code flag "P" broken out or distinctive signal displayed.
	Starting Signal	—	Both warning and preparatory signals lowered.

In System 1, when classes are *started:*

   (i)   at ten-minute intervals—
            the warning signal for each succeeding class shall be broken out or displayed at the starting signal of the preceding class.

(ii)   at five-minute intervals—
the preparatory signal for the first class to *start* shall be left displayed until the last class *starts*. The warning signal for each succeeding class shall be broken out or displayed at the preparatory signal of the preceding class.

or

System 2   Warning Signal   — White or yellow shape or flag.

Preparatory Signal   — Blue shape or flag.

Starting Signal   — Red shape or flag.

In System 2, each signal shall be lowered one minute before the next is made.
Class flags when used shall be broken out not later than the preparatory signal for each class.
When classes are *started:*

(i)   at ten-minute intervals—
the starting signal for each class shall be the warning signal for the next.

(ii)   at five-minute intervals—
the preparatory signal for each class shall be the warning signal for the next.

(b)   Although rules 4.1 "P" and 4.4(a) specify five-minute intervals, the sailing instructions may prescribe any intervals.

(c)   A warning signal shall not be made before its scheduled time, except with the consent of all yachts entitled to *race*.

(d)   When a significant error is made in the timing of the interval between any of the signals for starting a race, the recommended procedure is to signal a general recall, *postponement* or *abandonment* of the race whose start is directly affected by the error and a corresponding *postponement* of succeeding races. Unless otherwise prescribed in the sailing instructions, a new warning signal shall be made. When the race is not recalled, *postponed* or *abandoned* after an error in the timing of the interval, each succeeding signal shall be made at the correct interval from the preceding signal.

VISUAL STARTING SIGNALS TO GOVERN
Times shall be taken from the visual starting signals, and a failure or mistiming of a gun or other sound signal calling attention to starting signals shall be disregarded.

Designating the Course, Altering the Course or Race

Before or with the warning signal for a class that has not *started*, the race committee:

(a) shall either signal or otherwise designate the course.

(b) may remove and substitute a new course signal.

5.2 Before the preparatory signal, the race committee may shift a starting *mark*.

5.3 Before the starting signal, the race committee may:

(a) shorten the course to one prescribed in the sailing instructions.

(b) *postpone* to designate a new course before or with the new warning signal, or for any other reason.

(c) *postpone* to a later day.

(d) *cancel* the race for any reason.

5.4 After the starting signal, the race committee may:

(a) *abandon* and re-sail the race when there is an error in starting procedure.

(b) when prescribed in the sailing instructions, change the course at any rounding *mark* subject to proper notice being given to each yacht before she begins the changed leg.

(c) shorten the course by finishing a race at any rounding *mark* or as prescribed in the sailing instructions, or *abandon* or *cancel* the race:

  (i) because of foul weather, or

  (ii) because of insufficient wind making it improbable that the race will finish within the time limit, or

  (iii) because a *mark* is missing or has shifted, or

  (iv) for any other reasons directly affecting the safety or fairness of the competition.

5.5 After a race has been completed, the race committee shall not *abandon* or *cancel* it without taking the appropriate action under rule 74.2(b), Consideration of Redress.

5.6 The race committee shall notify all yachts concerned by signal or otherwise when and where a race *postponed* to a later day or *abandoned* will be *sailed*.

6 Starting and Finishing Lines

Unless otherwise prescribed in the sailing instructions, the starting and finishing lines shall be either:

(a) a line between a *mark* and a mast or staff on the committee boat or station clearly identified in the sailing instructions; or

(b) a line between two *marks*; or

(c) the extension of a line through two stationary posts, with or without a *mark* at or near its outer limit, inside which the yachts shall pass.

For types (a) and (c) of starting or finishing lines the sailing instructions may also prescribe that a *mark* will be laid at or near the inner end of the line, in which case yachts shall pass between it and the outer *mark*.

7   Start of a Race

7.1 STARTING AREA
The sailing instructions may define a starting area that may be bounded by buoys; if so, they shall not rank as *marks*.

7.2 TIMING THE START
The *start* of a yacht shall be timed from her starting signal.

8   Recalls

8.1 INDIVIDUAL RECALL
Unless otherwise prescribed in the sailing instructions, when, at her starting signal, any part of a yacht's hull, crew or equipment is on the course side of the starting line or its extensions, or she has not complied with rule 51.1(c), Sailing the Course, the race committee shall promptly display Code flag "X", accompanied by one sound signal, until all such yachts are wholly on the pre-start side of the starting line or its extensions and have complied with rule 51.1(c) when applicable, or for four minutes after the starting signal, whichever is the earlier. The sailing instructions may prescribe that the race committee will also hail the yacht's sail number.

8.2 GENERAL RECALL
(a) When there is either a number of unidentified premature starters or an error in starting procedure, the race committee may make a general recall signal in accordance with rules 4.1 "First Substitute", Visual Signals, and 4.3, Calling Attention to Visual Signals.

(b) Except as provided in rule 31.2, Rule Infringement, rule infringements before the preparatory signal for the new start shall be disregarded for the purpose of competing in the race to be re-started.

9   Marks

9.1 MARK MISSING
(a) When any *mark* either is missing or has shifted, the race committee shall, when possible, replace it in its stated position, or substitute a new one with similar characteristics or a buoy or vessel displaying Code flag "M" - the *mark* signal.

(b) When it is impossible either to replace the *mark* or to substitute a new one in time for the yachts to round or pass it, the race committee may, at its discretion, act in accordance with rule 5.4(c)(iii), Designating the Course, Altering the Course or Race.

9.2 MARK UNSEEN
When races are *sailed* in fog or at night, dead reckoning alone need not necessarily be accepted as evidence that a *mark* has been rounded or passed.

10 Finishing Within a Time Limit

Unless otherwise prescribed in the sailing instructions, in races where there is a time limit, one yacht *finishing* within the prescribed limit shall make the race valid for all other yachts in that race.

11 Ties

When there is a tie at the finish of a race, either actual or on corrected times, the points for the place for which the yachts have tied and for the place immediately below shall be added together and divided equally. When two or more yachts tie for a trophy or prize in either a single race or a series, the yachts so tied shall, when practicable, *sail* a deciding race; if not, either the tie shall be broken by a method established under rule 3.2(a)(viii), Sailing Instructions, or the yachts so tied shall either receive equal prizes or share the prize.

12 Races to be Re-sailed

When a race is to be re-sailed:

(a) All yachts entered in the original race shall be eligible to *start* in the race to be re-sailed.

(b) Subject to the entry requirements of the original race, and at the discretion of the race committee, new entries may be accepted.

(c) Rule infringements in the original race shall be disregarded for the purpose of competing in the race to be re-sailed.

(d) The race committee shall notify the yachts concerned when and where the race will be re-sailed.

(Numbers 13, 14, 15, 16 and 17 are spare numbers)

Part III—General Requirements

Owner's Responsibilities for Qualifying his Yacht

*A yacht intending to **race** shall, to avoid subsequent disqualification, comply with the rules of Part III before her preparatory signal and, when applicable, while **racing**.*

18 Entries

Unless otherwise prescribed either in the notice of race or in the sailing instructions, entries shall be made in the following form:

FORM OF ENTRY

To the Secretary . . . .*Club*
  Please enter the yacht . . . .*for*
the . . . .*race, on the* . . . .
her national letters and sail number are. . . . .
her rig is. . . . .
the colour of her hull is . . . .
and her rating or class is . . . .

  I agree to be bound by the racing rules of the IYRU, by the prescriptions of the national authority under which this race is sailed, by the sailing instructions and by the class rules.

Name	. . . .
Address	. . . .
Telephone No.	. . . .
Club	. . . .
Address during event	. . . .
Telephone No.	. . . .

Signed. . . . .*Date* . . . .
  (Owner or owner's representative)
Entrance fee enclosed

19 Measurement or Rating Certificates

19.1 Every yacht entering a race shall hold such valid measurement or rating certificate as is required by the national authority or other duly authorised body, by her class rules, by the notice of race, or by the sailing instructions.

19.2 An owner shall be responsible for maintaining his yacht in accordance with her class rules and for ensuring that her certificate is not invalidated by alterations. Deviations in excess of tolerances specified in the class rules caused by normal wear or damage and that do not affect the performance of the yacht shall not invalidate the measurement or rating certificate of the yacht for a particular race, but shall be rectified before she *races* again, unless in the opinion of the race committee there has been no practicable opportunity to rectify the wear or damage.

19.3 (a) The owner of a yacht who cannot produce such a certificate when required, may be permitted to sign and lodge with the race committee, before she *starts*, a statement in the following form:

To the Secretary .... *Club*

UNDERTAKING TO PRODUCE CERTIFICATE

The yacht ....*competes in the* ....
race on condition that a valid certificate previously issued by the authorised administrative body, or a copy of it, is submitted to the race committee before the end of the series, and that she competes in the race(s) on the measurement or rating of that certificate.

   Signed ....
   (Owner or his representative)
   Date ....

   (b) In this event the sailing instructions may require that the owner shall lodge such a deposit as may be required by the organising authority, which may be forfeited when such certificate or copy is not submitted to the race committee within the prescribed period.

20   Ownership of Yachts

20.1 A yacht shall be eligible to compete only when she is either owned by or on charter to and has been entered by a yacht or sailing club recognised by its national authority or a member or members thereof.

20.2 Two or more yachts owned or chartered wholly or in part by the same body or person shall not compete in the same race without the previous consent of the race committee.

20.3 An owner shall not steer any yacht other than his own in a race wherein his own yacht competes without the previous consent of the race committee.

21   Member on Board

Every yacht shall have on board a member of a yacht or sailing club recognised by its national authority to be in charge of the yacht as owner or owner's representative.

22 Shifting Ballast

22.1 GENERAL RESTRICTIONS
Floorboards shall be kept down; bulkheads and doors left standing; ladders, stairways and water tanks left in place; all cabin, galley and forecastle fixtures and fittings kept on board; all movable ballast shall be properly stowed under the floorboards or in lockers and no dead weight shall be shifted.

22.2 SHIPPING, UNSHIPPING OR SHIFTING BALLAST; WATER
From 2100 on the day before the race until she is no longer *racing,* a yacht shall not ship, unship or shift ballast, whether movable or fixed, or take in or discharge water, except for ordinary ship's use and the removal of bilge water. This rule shall not apply to wearing or carrying clothing, equipment or ballast in compliance with rule 61, Clothing and Equipment.

23 Anchor

Unless otherwise prescribed by her class rules, every yacht shall carry on board an anchor and chain or rope of suitable size.

24 Life-Saving Equipment

Unless otherwise prescribed by her class rules, every yacht shall carry adequate life-saving equipment for all persons on board, one item of which shall be ready for immediate use.

25 Class Insignia, National Letters and Sail Numbers

25.1 Every yacht of an international class recognised by the IYRU shall carry on her mainsail and, as provided in rule 25.3(c), on her spinnaker:

(a) The insignia denoting the class to which she belongs.

(b) A letter or letters showing her nationality, thus:

A	Argentina	CY	Sri Lanka	F	France
AE	Dubai	CZ	Czechoslovakia	FL	Liechtenstein
AL	Algeria	D	Denmark	G	Federal
ANU	Antigua	DDR	German		Republic of
AR	Egypt		Democratic		Germany
B	Belgium		Republic	GM	Guam
BA	Bahamas	DJ	Djibouti	GR	Greece
BH	Bahrain	DK	Democratic	GU	Guatemala
BL	Brazil		People's	H	Holland
BR	Burma		Republic of	HA	Netherlands
BU	Bulgaria		Korea		Antilles
CB	Colombia	DR	Dominican	I	Italy
CH	China		Republic	IL	Iceland
CI	Grand Cayman	E	Spain	IND	India
CP	Cyprus	EC	Ecuador	IR	Ireland

IS	Israel	MO	Monaco	SA	South Africa
J	Japan	MT	Malta	SE	Senegal
K	United	MX	Mexico	SM	San Marino
	Kingdom	MY	Malaysia	SR	Union of
KA	Australia	N	Norway		Soviet
KB	Bermuda	OE	Austria		Socialist
KBA	Barbados	OM	Oman		Republics
KC	Canada	P	Portugal	TA	Chinese
KF	Fiji	PH	Philippines		Taipei
KH	Hong Kong	PK	Pakistan	TH	Thailand
KJ	Jamaica	PR	Puerto Rico	TK	Turkey
KK	Kenya	PU	Peru	TN	Tunisia
KP	Papua New	PY	Paraguay	U	Uruguay
	Guinea	PZ	Poland	US	United
KS	Singapore	Q	Kuwait		States of
KT	Trinidad and	QA	Qatar		America
	Tobago	RB	Botswana	V	Venezuela
KV	British Virgin Is	RC	Cuba	VI	U.S. Virgin
KZ	New Zealand	RI	Indonesia		Is.
L	Finland	RK	Republic of	X	Chile
LX	Luxembourg		Korea	Y	Yugoslavia
M	Hungary	RM	Roumania	Z	Switzerland
MA	Morocco	S	Sweden	ZB	Zimbabwe

National letters need not be carried in home waters, except in an international championship.

(c) (i) A sail number allotted to her by her national authority or, when so prescribed by the class rules, by the international class association.

(ii) When so prescribed by the class rules, an owner may be allotted a personal sail number by the relevant issuing authority, which may be used on all his yachts in that class instead of the sail numbers allotted to such yachts in accordance with rule 25.1(c)(i).

25.2 The following specifications and minimum sizes of national letters and sail numbers shall apply.

(a) They shall be:

(i) clearly visible, legible and, unless otherwise prescribed by the class rules, of a single colour that strongly contrasts with the sail, and

(ii) in roman style (upright), without serifs, with arabic numerals, and with lines that are continuous and of uniform thickness.

(b) The minimum sizes for national letters and sail numbers shall be related to the yacht's overall length (LOA) and shall be as follows:

LOA	Height	Width excl. number 1 and letter I	Thickness	Space between adjoining letters & nos.
Under 3.5 m	230 mm	150 mm	30 mm	45 mm
3.5 m - 8.5 m	300 mm	200 mm	40 mm	60 mm
8.5 m - 11 m	375 mm	250 mm	50 mm	75 mm
Over 11 m	450 mm	300 mm	60 mm	90 mm

The size and style requirements of rules 25.2(a) and (b) shall not apply to sails made prior to 1st May, 1989.

(c) National letters shall be placed in front of or above the sail numbers. When the national letters end in "I" (e.g. Italy, U.S. Virgin Islands) and are placed in front of the numbers, they shall be separated from them by a horizontal line approximately 50 mm long.

25.3 The following positioning of class insignia, national letters and sail numbers on the sail shall apply.

(a) Unless otherwise prescribed by the class rules, the class insignia, national letter(s) and sail numbers shall be above an imaginary line projecting at right angles to the luff from a point one-third of the distance, measured from the tack, to the head of the sail; and shall be placed at different heights on the two sides of the sail, those on the starboard side being uppermost.

(b) Where the class insignia is of such a design that, when placed back to back on the two sides of the sail, they coincide, they may be so placed.

(c) The national letters and sail numbers only shall be similarly placed on both sides of the spinnaker, but at approximately half-height.

25.4 Other yachts shall comply with the rules of their national authority or class in regard to the allotment, carrying and size of insignia, letters and numbers, which rules shall, when practicable, conform to the above requirements.

25.5 When so prescribed in the notice of race or in the sailing instructions, a yacht chartered or loaned for an event may carry national letters or sail numbers in contravention of her class rules. In all other respects the sails shall comply with the class rules.

25.6 A yacht shall not be disqualified for infringing the provisions of rule 25 without prior warning and adequate opportunity to make correction.

26 Event Classification; Advertising

A yacht and her crew shall compete in conformity with Appendix 14, Event Classification and Advertising.

27 Forestays and Jib Tacks

Unless otherwise prescribed by the class rules, forestays and jib tacks (not including spinnaker staysails when not *close-hauled*) shall be fixed approximately in the centre-line of the yacht.

(Numbers 28, 29 and 30 are spare numbers)

Part IV—Right of Way Rules

Rights and Obligations when Yachts Meet

The rules of Part IV do not apply in any way to a vessel that is neither intending to **race** *nor* **racing;** *such vessel shall be treated in accordance with the International Regulations for Preventing Collisions at Sea or Government Right of Way Rules applicable to the area concerned. The rules of Part IV apply only between yachts that are either intending to* **race** *or are* **racing** *in the same or different races, and, except when rule 3.2(b)(xxix), Race Continues After Sunset, applies, replace the International Regulations for Preventing Collisions at Sea or Government Right of Way Rules applicable to the area concerned, from the time a yacht intending to* **race** *begins to* **sail** *about in the vicinity of the starting line until she has either* **finished** *or retired and has left the vicinity of the course. (See Appendix 9).*

SECTION A—Obligations and Penalties

31   Rule Infringement

31.1   A yacht may be penalised for infringing a rule of Part IV only when the infringement occurs while she is *racing.*

31.2   A yacht may be penalised, before or after she is *racing,* for seriously hindering a yacht that is *racing* or for infringing the sailing instructions.

32   Serious Damage

32.1   AVOIDING COLLISIONS
When a collision has resulted in serious damage, the right-of-way yacht shall be penalised as well as the other yacht when she had the opportunity but failed to make a reasonable attempt to avoid the collision.

32.2   HAILING
Except when *luffing* under rule 38.1, Luffing Rights, a right-of-way yacht that does not hail before or when making an alteration of course that may not be foreseen by the other yacht may be penalised as well as the yacht required to keep clear when a collision resulting in serious damage occurs.

33   Contact between Yachts Racing

When there is contact that is not both minor and unavoidable between the hulls, equipment or crew of two yachts, both shall be penalised unless: either

(a)   one of the yachts retires in acknowledgement of the infringement, or exonerates herself by accepting an alternative penalty when so prescribed in the sailing instructions,

or

(b)   one or both of these yachts lodges a valid **protest**.

34   Maintaining Rights

When a yacht that may have infringed a **rule** does not retire or exonerate herself, other yachts shall continue to accord her such rights as she has under the rules of Part IV.

SECTION B—Principal Right of Way Rules and their Limitations

These rules apply except when over-ridden by a rule in Section C.

35   Limitations on Altering Course

When one yacht is required to keep clear of another, the right-of-way yacht shall not alter course so as to prevent the other yacht from keeping clear, or so as to obstruct her while she is keeping clear, except:

(a)   to the extent permitted by rule 38.1, Luffing Rights, and

(b)   when assuming a *proper course:*
      either

      (i)   to *start*, unless subject to rule 40, Same Tack, Luffing before Clearing the Starting Line, or to the second part of rule 44.1(b), Returning to Start,

      or

      (ii)   when rounding a *mark*.

36   Opposite Tacks - Basic Rule

A *port-tack* yacht shall keep clear of a *starboard-tack* yacht.

37   Same Tack - Basic Rules

37.1   WHEN OVERLAPPED
A *windward yacht* shall keep clear of a *leeward yacht*.

37.2   WHEN NOT OVERLAPPED
A yacht *clear astern* shall keep clear of a yacht *clear ahead*.

37.3   TRANSITIONAL
A yacht that establishes an *overlap* to *leeward* from *clear astern* shall initially allow the *windward yacht* ample room and opportunity to keep clear.

38   Same Tack - Luffing after Clearing the Starting Line

38.1 LUFFING RIGHTS
After she has *started* and cleared the starting line, a yacht *clear ahead* or a *leeward yacht* may *luff* as she pleases, subject to the following limitations of this rule.

38.2 LIMITATIONS

(a) Proper Course Limitations:
A *leeward yacht* shall not *sail* above her *proper course* while an *overlap* exists, if when the *overlap* began or at any time during its existence, the helmsman of the *windward yacht* (when sighting abeam from his normal station and *sailing* no higher than the *leeward yacht*) has been abreast or forward of the mainmast of the *leeward yacht*.

(b) Overlap Limitations:
For the purpose of rule 38 only: An *overlap* does not exist unless the yachts are clearly within two overall lengths of the longer yacht; and an *overlap* that exists between two yachts when the leading yacht *starts*, or when one or both of them completes a *tack* or *gybe*, shall be regarded as a new *overlap* beginning at that time.

(c) Hailing to Stop or Prevent a Luff:
When there is doubt, the *leeward yacht* may assume that she has the right to *luff* or *sail* above her *proper course* unless the helmsman of the *windward yacht* has hailed either:

(i)   "Mast Abeam", or words to that effect, or

(ii)   "Obstruction", or words to that effect.

The *leeward yacht* shall be governed by such hail and curtail her *luff*. When she deems the hail improper, her only remedy is to protest.

(d) Curtailing a Luff:
The *windward yacht* shall not cause a *luff* to be curtailed because of her proximity to the *leeward yacht* unless an *obstruction*, a third yacht or other object restricts her ability to respond.

(e) Luffing Rights over Two or More Yachts:
A yacht shall not *luff* unless she has the right to *luff* all yachts that would be affected by her *luff*, in which case they shall all respond, even when an intervening yacht or yachts would not otherwise have the right to *luff*.

39   Same Tack - Sailing below a Proper Course after Starting

A yacht that is on a free leg of the course shall not *sail* below her *proper course* when she is clearly within three of her overall lengths of a *leeward yacht* or of a yacht *clear astern* that is steering a course to *leeward* of her own.

40 Same Tack - Luffing before Clearing the Starting Line

Before a yacht *clear ahead* or a *leeward yacht* has *started* and cleared the starting line, any *luff* on her part that causes another yacht to have to alter course to avoid a collision shall be carried out slowly and initially in such a way as to give a *windward yacht* room and opportunity to keep clear. Furthermore, the *leeward yacht* shall not so *luff* above a *close-hauled* course while the helmsman of the *windward yacht* (sighting abeam from his normal station) is abreast or forward of the mainmast of the *leeward yacht*. Rules 38.2(c), Hailing to Stop or Prevent a Luff; 38.2(d), Curtailing a Luff; and 38.2(e), Luffing Rights over Two or More Yachts, also apply.

41 Changing Tacks - Tacking and Gybing

41.1 BASIC RULE
A yacht that is either *tacking* or *gybing* shall keep clear of a yacht *on a tack*.

41.2 TRANSITIONAL
A yacht shall neither *tack* nor *gybe* into a position that will give her right of way unless she does so far enough from a yacht *on a tack* to enable this yacht to keep clear without having to begin to alter her course until after the *tack* or *gybe* has been completed.

41.3 ONUS
A yacht that *tacks* or *gybes* has the onus of satisfying the **protest committee** that she completed her *tack* or *gybe* in accordance with rule 41.2.

41.4 WHEN SIMULTANEOUS
When two yachts are both *tacking* or both *gybing* at the same time, the one on the other's port side shall keep clear.

SECTION C—Rules that Apply at Marks and Obstructions and other Exceptions to the Rules of Section B

When a rule of this section applies, to the extent to which it explicitly provides rights and obligations, it over-rides any conflicting rule of Section B, Principal Right of Way Rules and their Limitations, except rule 35, Limitations on Altering Course.

42 Rounding or Passing Marks and Obstructions

Rule 42 applies when yachts are about to round or pass a *mark* on the same required side or an *obstruction* on the same side, except that it shall not apply:

(a) between two yachts on opposite *tacks*:

(i)   when they are on a beat, or

(ii)   when one, but not both, of them will have to *tack* either to round or pass the *mark* or to avoid the *obstruction*, or

(b) when rule 42.4 applies.

42.1 WHEN OVERLAPPED

An Outside Yacht

(a) An outside yacht shall give each inside *overlapping* yacht room to round or pass the *mark* or *obstruction*, except as provided in rule 42.3. Room is the space needed by an inside *overlapping* yacht that is handled in a seamanlike manner in the prevailing conditions to pass in safety between an outside yacht and a *mark* or *obstruction*, and includes space to *tack* or *gybe* when either is an integral part of the rounding or passing manoeuvre.

(b) An outside yacht *overlapped* when she comes within two of her overall lengths of a *mark* or *obstruction* shall give room as required, even though the *overlap* may thereafter be broken.

(c) An outside yacht that claims to have broken an *overlap* has the onus of satisfying the **protest committee** that she became *clear ahead* when she was more than two of her overall lengths from the *mark* or *obstruction*.

An Inside Yacht

(d) A yacht that claims an inside *overlap* has the onus of satisfying the **protest committee** that she established the *overlap* in accordance with rule 42.3.

(e) When an inside yacht of two or more *overlapped* yachts, either on opposite *tacks* or on the same *tack* without *luffing* rights, will have to *gybe* in order most directly to assume a *proper course* to the next *mark*, she shall *gybe* at the first reasonable opportunity.

Hailing

(f) A yacht that hails when claiming the establishment or termination of an *overlap* or insufficiency of room at a *mark* or *obstruction* thereby helps to support her claim.

42.2 WHEN NOT OVERLAPPED

A Yacht Clear Astern

(a) A yacht *clear astern* when the yacht *clear ahead* comes within two of her overall lengths of a *mark* or *obstruction* shall keep clear in anticipation of and during the rounding or passing manoeuvre, whether the yacht *clear ahead* remains on the same *tack* or *gybes*.

(b) A yacht *clear astern* shall not *luff* above *close-hauled* so as to prevent a yacht *clear ahead* from *tacking* to round a *mark*.

A Yacht Clear Ahead

(c) A yacht *clear ahead* that *tacks* to round a *mark* is subject to rule 41, Changing Tacks - Tacking and Gybing.

(d) A yacht *clear ahead* shall be under no obligation to give room to a yacht *clear astern* before an *overlap* is established.

42.3 LIMITATIONS

(a) Limitation on Establishing an Overlap
A yacht that establishes an inside *overlap* from *clear astern* is entitled to room under rule 42.1(a) only when, at that time, the outside yacht:

(i)   is able to give room, and

(ii)   is more than two of her overall lengths from the *mark* or *obstruction*. However, when a yacht completes a *tack* within two of her overall lengths of a *mark* or *obstruction*, she shall give room as required by rule 42.1(a) to a yacht that, by *luffing*, cannot thereafter avoid establishing a late inside *overlap*.

At a continuing *obstruction*, rule 42.3(b) applies.

(b) Limitation When an Obstruction is a Continuing One.
A yacht *clear astern* may establish an *overlap* between a yacht *clear ahead* and a continuing *obstruction*, such as a shoal or the shore or another vessel, only when, at that time, there is room for her to pass between them in safety.

42.4 AT A STARTING MARK SURROUNDED BY NAVIGABLE WATER
When approaching the starting line to *start* until clearing the starting *marks* after *starting*, a *leeward yacht* shall be under no obligation to give any *windward yacht* room to pass to leeward of a starting *mark* surrounded by navigable water, including such a *mark* that is also an *obstruction*; but, after the starting signal, a *leeward yacht* shall not deprive a *windward yacht* of room at such a *mark* by *sailing* either:

(a) to windward of the compass bearing of the course to the next *mark*, or

(b) above *close-hauled*.

43   Close-Hauled, Hailing for Room to Tack at Obstructions

43.1 HAILING
When two *close-hauled* yachts are on the same *tack* and safe pilotage requires the yacht *clear ahead* or the *leeward yacht* to make a substantial alteration of course to clear an *obstruction*, and when she intends to *tack*, but cannot *tack* without colliding with the other yacht, she shall hail the other yacht for room to *tack* and clear the other yacht, but she shall not hail and *tack* simultaneously.

43.2 RESPONDING

The hailed yacht at the earliest possible moment after the hail shall either:

(a) *tack*, in which case the hailing yacht shall begin to *tack* immediately she is able to *tack* and clear the other yacht; or

(b) reply "You *tack*", or words to that effect, in which case:

    (i) the hailing yacht shall immediately *tack* and

    (ii) the hailed yacht shall give the hailing yacht room to *tack* and clear her.

    (iii) The onus of satisfying the **protest committee** that she gave sufficient room shall lie on the hailed yacht that replied "You *tack*".

43.3 WHEN AN OBSTRUCTION IS ALSO A MARK

(a) When an *obstruction* is a starting *mark* surrounded by navigable water, or the ground tackle of such a *mark*, and when approaching the starting line to *start* and after *starting*, the yacht *clear ahead* or the *leeward yacht* shall not be entitled to room to *tack*.

(b) At other *obstructions* that are *marks*, when the hailed yacht can fetch the *obstruction*, the hailing yacht shall not be entitled to room to *tack* and clear the hailed yacht, and the hailed yacht shall immediately so inform the hailing yacht. When, thereafter, the hailing yacht again hails for room to *tack* and clear the hailed yacht, the hailed yacht shall, at the earliest possible moment after the hail, give the hailing yacht the required room. After receiving room, the hailing yacht shall either retire immediately or exonerate herself by accepting an alternative penalty when so prescribed in the sailing instructions.

(c) When, after having refused to respond to a hail under rule 43.3(b), the hailed yacht fails to fetch, she shall retire immediately or exonerate herself by accepting an alternative penalty when so prescribed in the sailing instructions.

44 Returning to Start

44.1

(a) After the starting signal, a premature starter returning to *start*, or a yacht working into position from the course side of the starting line or its extensions, shall keep clear of all yachts that are *starting* or have *started* correctly, until she is wholly on the pre-start side of the starting line or its extensions.

(b) Thereafter, she shall be accorded the rights under the rules of Part IV of a yacht that is *starting* correctly; but when she thereby acquires right of way over another yacht that is *starting* correctly, she shall allow that yacht ample room and opportunity to keep clear.

44.2 A premature starter, while continuing to *sail* the course and until it is obvious that she is returning to *start*, shall be accorded the rights under the rules of Part IV of a yacht that has *started*.

45 Keeping Clear after Touching a Mark

45.1 A yacht that has touched a *mark* and is exonerating herself shall keep clear of all other yachts until she has completed her exoneration and, when she has *started*, is on a *proper course* to the next *mark*.

45.2 A yacht that has touched a *mark*, while continuing to *sail* the course and until it is obvious that she is exonerating herself, shall be accorded rights under the rules of Part IV.

46 Person Overboard; Yacht Anchored, Aground or Capsized

46.1 A yacht under way shall keep clear of another yacht *racing* that:

(a) is manoeuvring or hailing for the purpose of rescuing a person overboard, or

(b) is anchored, aground or capsized.

46.2 A yacht shall not be penalised when she is unable to avoid fouling a yacht that she is attempting to assist or that goes aground or is capsized.

46.3 A yacht is capsized from the time her masthead is in the water until her masthead is clear of the water and she has steerage way.

46.4 A yacht anchored or aground shall indicate the fact to any yacht that may be in danger of fouling her. Under normal conditions, a hail is sufficient indication. Of two yachts anchored, the one that anchored later shall keep clear, except that a yacht dragging shall keep clear of one that is not.

(Numbers 47, 48 and 49 are spare numbers)

Part V—Other Sailing Rules

Obligations in Handling a Yacht

*A yacht is subject to the rules of Part V only while she is **racing.***

50 Ranking as a Starter

A yacht whose entry has been accepted and that *sails* about in the vicinity of the starting line between her preparatory and starting signals shall rank as a starter whether she *starts* or not.

51 Sailing the Course

51.1 (a) A yacht shall *start* and *finish* only as prescribed in the starting and finishing definitions.

(b) When any part of a yacht's hull, crew or equipment is on the course side of the starting line or its extensions at the starting signal, she shall thereafter *start* in accordance with the definition.

(c) When Code flag "I" has been displayed, and when any part of a yacht's hull, crew or equipment is on the course side of the starting line or its extensions during the minute before her starting signal, she shall *sail* to the pre-start side of the line across one of its extensions and *start*.

(d) Failure of a yacht to see or hear her recall signal shall not relieve her of her obligation to *start* correctly.

51.2 A yacht shall *sail* the course so as to round or pass each *mark* on the required side in correct sequence, and so that a string representing her wake, from the time she *starts* until she *finishes*, would, when drawn taut, lie on the required side of each *mark*, touching each rounding *mark*.

51.3 A *mark* has a required side for a yacht as long as she is on a leg that it begins, bounds or ends. A starting line *mark* begins to have a required side for a yacht when she *starts*. A starting limit *mark* has a required side for a yacht from the time she is approaching the starting line to *start* until she has left the *mark* astern on the first leg. A finishing line *mark* and a finishing limit *mark* cease to have a required side for a yacht when she *finishes*.

51.4 A yacht that rounds or passes a *mark* on the wrong side may exonerate herself by making her course conform to the requirements of rule 51.2.

51.5 It is not necessary for a yacht to cross the finishing line completely; after *finishing*, she may clear it in either direction.

52 Touching a Mark

52.1 A yacht shall neither:

    (a) touch:

        (i) a starting *mark* before *starting*, or

        (ii) a *mark* that begins, bounds or ends the leg of the course on which she is *sailing*, or

        (iii) a finishing *mark* after *finishing* and before clearing the finishing line and *marks*,

    nor

    (b) cause a *mark* or *mark* vessel to shift to avoid being touched.

52.2 (a) When a yacht infringes rule 52.1, she may exonerate herself by *sailing* well clear of all other yachts as soon as possible after the incident, and remaining clear while she makes two complete 360° turns (720°) in the same direction, including two *tacks* and two *gybes*.

    (b) When a yacht touches a finishing *mark*, she shall not rank as having *finished* until she first completes her turns and thereafter *finishes*.

52.3 When a yacht is wrongfully compelled by another yacht to infringe rule 52.1, she shall be exonerated:

    (a) by the retirement of the other yacht (or by the other yacht accepting an alternative penalty when so prescribed in the sailing instructions) in acknowledgement of the infringement, or

    (b) in accordance with rule 74.4(b), Penalties and Exoneration, after lodging a valid **protest**.

53 Casting Off, Anchoring, Making Fast and Hauling Out

53.1 AT THE PREPARATORY SIGNAL
A yacht shall be afloat and off moorings at her preparatory signal, but may be anchored.

53.2 WHEN RACING
A yacht may anchor, but shall not make fast or be made fast by means other than anchoring, nor be hauled out, except for the purpose of rule 55, Aground or Foul of an Obstruction, or to effect repairs, reef sails or bail out.

53.3 MEANS OF ANCHORING
Means of anchoring may include the crew standing on the bottom or any weight lowered to the bottom. A yacht shall recover any anchor or weight used, and any chain or rope attached to it, before continuing in the race, unless, after making every effort, she fails to do so. In this case she shall

report the circumstances to the race committee, which may penalise her when it considers the loss due either to inadequate gear or to insufficient effort to recover it.

54   Propulsion

54.1 BASIC RULE
Except when permitted by rule 54.3, a yacht shall compete only by *sailing*, and her crew shall not otherwise move their bodies to propel the yacht. Fundamental Rule A, Rendering Assistance, and rule 55, Aground or Foul of an Obstruction, over-ride rule 54.

54.2 PROHIBITED ACTIONS
Without limiting the application of rule 54.1, these actions are prohibited:

(a) pumping—repeated fanning of any sail either by trimming and releasing the sail or by vertical or athwartships body movement;

(b) rocking—repeated rolling of the yacht induced either by body movement or adjustment of the sails or centreboard;

(c) ooching—sudden forward body movement, stopped abruptly;

(d) sculling—repeated movement of the helm not necessary for steering;

(e) repeated *tacks* or *gybes* unrelated to changes in the wind or to tactical considerations.

54.3 EXCEPTIONS

(a) Immediately before, during and immediately after a *tack* or *gybe*, the yacht's crew may move their bodies to roll the yacht, provided that such movements do not:

(i)   advance the yacht further in the race than she would have advanced in the absence of the *tack* or *gybe*, or

(ii)   move her mast away from the vertical more than once.

(b) On a free leg of the course, when surfing (rapidly accelerating down the leeward side of a wave) or planing is possible, the yacht's crew may, in order to initiate surfing or planing, pump the sheet, but not the guy, controlling any sail, but only once for each wave or gust of wind. When the mainsail is pumped, only that part of the sheet between the crew member handling the sheet and the first block on the boom shall be used.

(c) Class rules may alter or add to rule 54.3(b).

55   Aground or Foul of an Obstruction

A yacht, after grounding or fouling another vessel or other object, is subject to rule 57, Manual and Stored Power, and may, in getting clear, use her own anchors, boats, ropes, spars and other gear; may send out an anchor in a boat; may be refloated by her crew going overboard either to stand on the bottom or to go ashore to push off; but may receive outside assistance only from the crew of the vessel fouled. A yacht shall recover all her own gear used in getting clear before continuing in the race.

56 Sounding

Any means of sounding may be used, provided that rule 54, Propulsion, is not infringed.

57 Manual and Stored Power

A yacht's standing rigging, running rigging, spars and movable hull appendages shall be adjusted and operated by manual power only, and no device shall be used for these operations that derives assistance from stored energy for doing work. A power winch or windlass may be used in weighing anchor or in getting clear after running aground or fouling any object, and a power pump may be used in an auxiliary yacht.

58 Boarding

Unless otherwise prescribed in the sailing instructions, no person shall board a yacht, except for the purposes of Fundamental Rule A, Rendering Assistance, or to attend an injured or ill member of the crew or temporarily as one of the crew of a vessel fouled.

59 Leaving, Crew Overboard

Unless otherwise prescribed in the sailing instructions, no person on board a yacht when she begins *racing* shall leave, unless injured or ill, or for the purposes of Fundamental Rule A, Rendering Assistance, except that any member of the crew may fall overboard or leave her to swim, stand on the bottom as a means of anchoring, haul her out ashore to effect repairs, reef sails or bail out, or to help her to get clear after grounding or fouling another vessel or object, provided that this person is back on board before the yacht continues in the race.

60 Outside Assistance

Except as permitted by Fundamental Rule A, Rendering Assistance, rule 55, Aground or Foul of an Obstruction, and rule 58, Boarding, a yacht shall neither receive outside assistance nor use any gear other than that on board when her preparatory signal was made.

61 Clothing and Equipment

61.1 (a) Except as permitted by rule 61.2, a competitor shall not wear or carry clothing or equipment for the purpose of increasing his weight.

(b) Furthermore, the total weight of clothing and equipment worn or carried by a competitor shall not be capable of exceeding 15 kilograms, when soaked with water and weighed as provided in Appendix 10, Weighing of Wet Clothing, unless class rules or the sailing instructions prescribe a lesser or greater weight, in which case such weight shall apply, except that it shall not exceed 20 kilograms.

61.2 When so prescribed by the class rules, weight jackets of non-metallic material (excepting normal fasteners), with or without pockets, compartments or containers, shall be permitted, provided that the jacket:

(a) is permanently buoyant,

(b) does not extend more than 30 mm above the competitor's shoulders, and

(c) can be removed by the competitor in less than ten seconds,

and that ballast carried in the pockets, compartments and containers shall only be water. For the purpose of rule 61.1(b), the pockets, compartments and containers shall be filled completely with water and included in the total weight.

61.3 When a competitor is protested or selected for inspection, he shall produce all containers referred to in rule 61.2 that were carried while *racing*.

61.4 Unless otherwise prescribed in the sailing instructions, rule 61.1(b) shall not apply in events for cruiser-racer type yachts required to be equipped with lifelines.

62 Increasing Stability

(a) Unless otherwise prescribed by the class rules, a yacht shall not use any device, such as a trapeze or plank, to project outboard the weight of any of the crew.

(b) When lifelines are required by the class rules or the sailing instructions, no crew member shall station any part of his torso outside them, except when it is necessary to perform a task, and then only temporarily. On yachts equipped with upper and lower lifelines of wire, a crew member sitting on the deck facing outboard with his waist inside the lower lifeline may have the upper part of his body outside the upper lifeline.

63 Skin Friction

A yacht:

(a) shall not eject or release from a container any substance (such as polymer), or

(b) unless otherwise prescribed by her class rules, shall not have specially textured hull or appendage surfaces, the purpose of which is, or could be, to reduce the frictional resistance of her surface by altering the character of the flow of water inside the boundary layer.

64 Setting and Sheeting Sails

64.1 CHANGING SAILS

While changing headsails and spinnakers, a replacing sail may be fully set and trimmed before the sail it replaces is taken in, but only one mainsail and, except when changing, only one spinnaker shall be carried set.

64.2 SPINNAKER BOOMS

Only one spinnaker boom shall be used at a time and, when in use, shall be attached to and carried only on the side of the foremost mast opposite to the main boom and shall be fixed to the mast.

64.3 SPINNAKERS

A spinnaker, including a headsail set as a spinnaker, shall not be set without a boom. The tack of a spinnaker that is set and drawing shall be in close proximity to the outboard end of the spinnaker boom, except when hoisting, gybing or lowering the spinnaker.

64.4 USE OF OUTRIGGERS

(a) No sail shall be sheeted over or through an outrigger, except as permitted in rule 64.4(b). An outrigger is any fitting or other device so placed that it could exert outward pressure on a sheet or sail at a point from which, with the yacht upright, a vertical line would fall outside the hull or deck planking. For the purpose of this rule: bulwarks, rails and rubbing strakes are not part of the hull or deck planking. A boom of a boomed headsail that requires no adjustment when *tacking* is not an outrigger.

(b) (i) Any sail may be sheeted to or led above a boom regularly used for a working sail and permanently attached to the mast from which the head of the working sail is set.

(ii) A headsail may be sheeted or attached at its clew to a spinnaker boom, provided that a spinnaker is not set.

64.5 HEADSAILS

The following distinction shall apply between spinnakers and headsails. A headsail is a sail in which the mid-girth, measured from the mid-points of the luff and leech, does not exceed 50% of the length of the foot, and in which any other intermediate girth does not exceed a value similarly proportional to its distance from the head of the sail. A sail tacked down abaft the foremost mast is not a headsail.

64.6 CLASS RULES

Class rules may alter or add to this rule.

65   Flags

A national authority may prescribe the flag usage that shall be observed by yachts under its jurisdiction.

66   Fog Signals and Lights

Every yacht shall observe the International Regulations for Preventing Collisions at Sea or Government Rules for fog signals and, as a minimum, the exhibition of lights at night.

(Number 67 is a spare number)

Part VI—**Protests, Penalties and Appeals**

Definitions

*When a term defined below is used in its defined sense, it is printed in **bold** type. The definitions rank as rules.*

Rules -

(a) These racing rules,

(b) the prescriptions of the national authority concerned, when they apply,

(c) the sailing instructions,

(d) the appropriate class rules, and

(e) any other conditions governing the event.

Protest - An allegation by a yacht under rule 68, Protests by Yachts, that another yacht has infringed a **rule** or **rules.**

The term **protest** includes when appropriate:

(a) a request for redress under rule 69, Requests for Redress; or

(b) a request for a hearing under rule 70.1(c), Action by Race or Protest Committee, or Appendix 3, paragraph 2.6, Alternative Penalties; or

(c) a notification of a hearing under rule 70.2, Action by Race or Protest Committee; or

(d) an investigation of redress under rule 70.3, Yacht Materially Prejudiced; or

(e) a report by a measurer under rule 70.4, Measurer's Responsibility.

Parties to a Protest - The protesting yacht, the protested yacht and any other yacht involved in the incident that might be penalised as a result of the **protest;** and the race committee when it is involved in a **protest** pertaining to rule 69(a), Requests for Redress, or rule 70, Action by Race or Protest Committee.

Protest Committee - The body appointed to hear and decide **protests** in accordance with rule 1.4, Protest Committees, namely:

(a) the race committee or a sub-committee thereof; or

(b) a separate and independent protest committee or jury; or

(c) an international jury.

Interested Party - Anyone who stands to gain or lose as a result of a decision of a **protest committee** or who has a close personal interest in the result.

SECTION A—Initiation of Action

68   Protests by Yachts

68.1   RIGHT TO PROTEST
A yacht can protest any other yacht, except that a **protest** for an alleged infringement of the rules of Part IV can be made only by a yacht directly involved in or witnessing an incident.

68.2   INFORMING THE PROTESTED YACHT
A protesting yacht shall try to inform the yacht she intends to protest that a **protest** will be lodged. When an alternative penalty is prescribed in the sailing instructions, she shall hail the other yacht immediately.

68.3   DURING A RACE - PROTEST FLAG

(a)   An intention to protest an infringement of the **rules** occurring during a race shall be signified by the protesting yacht conspicuously displaying a flag. Code flag "B" is always acceptable, irrespective of any other provisions in the sailing instructions.

(b)   The flag shall be displayed at the first reasonable opportunity after the incident.

(c)   (i)   Except as provided in rule 68.3(c)(ii), the flag shall be displayed until the yacht *finishes* or, when the first opportunity occurs after *finishing*, until acknowledged by the race committee.

        (ii)   In the case of a yacht *sailed* single-handed, it will be sufficient to display the flag at the first reasonable opportunity after the incident and to have it acknowledged by the race committee when the protesting yacht *finishes*.

(d)   When the yacht retires, the flag shall be displayed until she has informed the race committee or has left the vicinity of the course.

68.4   EXCEPTION TO PROTEST FLAG REQUIREMENT
A yacht may protest without having displayed a protest flag when either:

(a)   she has no knowledge of the facts justifying a **protest** until she has *finished* or retired, or

(b)   having been a witness not directly involved in the incident, she learns that a yacht that displayed a protest flag has failed to lodge a valid **protest** in accordance with rule 33(b), Contact between Yachts Racing, or rule 52.3(b), Touching a Mark.

68.5 PARTICULARS TO BE INCLUDED

A **protest** shall be in writing and be signed by the owner or his representative, and include the following particulars:

(a) the identity of the yacht being protested;

(b) the date, time and whereabouts of the incident;

(c) the particular **rule** or **rules** alleged to have been infringed;

(d) a description of the incident;

(e) unless irrelevant, a diagram of the incident.

68.6 TIME LIMIT

A protesting yacht shall lodge her **protest** with the race committee:

(a) within two hours of the time she *finishes* the race or within such time as may have been prescribed in the sailing instructions, unless the **protest committee** has reason to extend this time limit, or

(b) when she does not *finish* the race, within such time as the **protest committee** considers reasonable in the circumstances.

68.7 FEE

Unless otherwise prescribed in the sailing instructions, a **protest** shall not be accompanied by a fee.

68.8 REMEDYING DEFECTS IN THE PROTEST

The **protest committee** shall allow the protesting yacht to remedy during the hearing:

(a) any defect in the particulars required by rule 68.5, provided that the **protest** identifies the nature of the incident, and

(b) a failure to deposit such fee as may be required under rule 68.7.

68.9 WITHDRAWING A PROTEST

When a written **protest** has been lodged, it shall not be withdrawn, but shall be decided by the **protest committee,** unless prior to the hearing one or more of the yachts acknowledges the infringement, except that, when the **protest committee** finds that contact between two yachts was minor and unavoidable, a protesting yacht may withdraw her **protest.**

69 Requests for Redress

A yacht that alleges that her finishing position has been materially prejudiced through no fault of her own by:

(a) an action or omission of the race committee or **protest committee,** or

(b) rendering assistance in accordance with Fundamental Rule A, Rendering Assistance, or

(c)   being damaged by another vessel that was required to keep clear, or |

(d)   a yacht infringing Fundamental Rule C, Fair Sailing, or against which a penalty has been imposed under rule 75.1, Penalties by the Race Committee or Protest Committee,

may request redress from the **protest committee** in accordance with the requirements for a **protest** provided in rules 68.5, 68.6, 68.7 and 68.8, Protests by Yachts. A protest flag need not be displayed. The **protest committee** shall then proceed in accordance with rule 74.2, Consideration of Redress.

70   Action by Race or Protest Committee

70.1   WITHOUT A HEARING

(a)   The race committee may act in accordance with rule 74.4, Penalties and Exoneration, without a hearing against a yacht that fails either to *start* or *finish*.

(b)   The **protest committee** may act as provided in rule 70.1(a) against a yacht that infringes rule 54.2 or 54.3, Propulsion.

(c)   A yacht so penalised shall be entitled to a hearing upon request, and shall be informed of the action taken, either by letter or notification in the race results, or by such other means as the sailing instructions may prescribe.

70.2   WITH A HEARING
The race committee or the **protest committee** may call a hearing when it:

(a)   sees an apparent infringement by a yacht of any of the **rules** (except as provided in rule 70.1), or

(b)   learns directly from a written or oral statement by a yacht (including one contained in an invalid **protest**) that she may have infringed a **rule,** or

(c)   has reasonable grounds for believing that an infringement resulted in serious damage, or

(d)   receives a report not later than the same day from a witness who was neither competing in the race nor otherwise an **interested party,** alleging an infringement, or

(e)   has reasonable grounds for supposing, from the evidence at the hearing of a valid **protest,** that any yacht involved in the incident may have committed an infringement.

For such hearings, the race committee or **protest committee** shall notify each yacht involved thereof in writing, delivered or mailed not later than 1800 on the day after:

(i)   the finish of the race, or

(iii) the hearing of the **protest**.

When rule 70.2(e) applies, or rule 70.2(b) after a **protest** has been declared |
invalid at a hearing, this notice may be given orally at the hearing. The
notice shall identify the incident, the **rule** or **rules** alleged to have been
infringed and the time and place of the hearing.

70.3   YACHT MATERIALLY PREJUDICED
The race committee or the **protest committee** may initiate consideration
of redress when it is satisfied that any of the circumstances set out in rule
69, Requests for Redress, may have occurred.

70.4   MEASURER'S RESPONSIBILITY
When a measurer concludes that a yacht does not comply with her class
rules or measurement or rating certificate:

(a) before a race: he shall request the owner or his representative to correct
the defect. When the defect is not corrected, he shall report the matter
in writing to the race committee, which shall reject or rescind the yacht's
entry or approve the entry in accordance with rule 19, Measurement
or Rating Certificates. The yacht shall be entitled to a hearing upon
request.

(b) after a race: he shall make a report to the race committee or to the
protest committee, which shall then notify the yacht concerned and
call a hearing.

The measurer shall not have the authority either to rescind an entry or to
disqualify a yacht.

SECTION B—Protest Procedure

71   **Procedural Requirements**

71.1   REQUIREMENT FOR A HEARING
A yacht shall not be penalised without a hearing, except as provided in
rule 70.1, Action by Race or Protest Committee.

71.2   INTERESTED PARTIES

(a) No member of a **protest committee** shall take part in the discussion
or decision upon any disputed question in which he is an **interested
party,** but this does not preclude him from giving evidence in such
a case.

(b) A **party to a protest** who wishes to object to a member of the **protest
committee** on the grounds that he is an **interested party** shall do so

before evidence is taken at the hearing or as soon thereafter as he
becomes aware of the conflict of interest.

71.3 PROTESTS BETWEEN YACHTS IN SEPARATE RACES
A **protest** occurring between yachts competing in separate races organised
by different clubs shall be heard by a combined committee of the clubs
concerned.

72 Notification of Parties

The **parties to the protest** shall be notified of the time and place of the
hearing, and the **protest**, or copies of it, shall be made available to them.
A reasonable time shall be allowed for the preparation of a defence.

73 Hearings

73.1 RIGHT TO BE PRESENT
The **parties to the protest,** or a representative of each, shall have the right
to be present throughout the hearing of all the evidence and to question
witnesses. When there is an alleged infringement of a rule of Parts IV or
V, the representatives of yachts shall have been on board at the time of
the incident, unless the **protest committee** has reasonable grounds for ruling
otherwise. Each witness, unless he is a member of the **protest committee,**
shall be excluded, except when giving his evidence. Others may be admitted
as observers at the discretion of the **protest committee.**

73.2 ACCEPTANCE OR REFUSAL OF A PROTEST
When the **protest committee** decides that the requirements of rule 68,
Protests by Yachts, and of the sailing instructions have been met, the **protest**
is valid, and the **protest committee** shall proceed with the hearing. When
these requirements are not met, the **protest** is invalid and shall be refused,
but such a decision shall not be reached without giving the protesting party
an opportunity of bringing evidence that all requirements have been met.

73.3 TAKING OF EVIDENCE
The **protest committee** shall take the evidence presented by the **parties
to the protest** and such other evidence as it deems necessary.

73.4 EVIDENCE OF COMMITTEE MEMBER
Any member of the **protest committee** who speaks of his own observation
of the incident shall give his evidence as a witness in the presence of the
parties to the protest, and may be questioned.

73.5 FAILURE TO ATTEND
Failure on the part of any **party to the protest,** or a representative, to make
an effort to attend the hearing may justify the **protest committee** in deciding
the **protest** as it thinks fit without a full hearing.

73.6 RE-OPENING A HEARING

(a) A hearing may be re-opened when the **protest committee** decides that it may have made a significant error or when material new evidence becomes available within a reasonable time. A **party to the protest** may request such a re-opening, provided that the request is lodged before 1800 on the day following the decision, unless the **protest committee** has reason to extend this time limit.

(b) When the hearing of a **protest** is re-opened, a majority of the members of the **protest committee** shall, when possible, be members of the original **protest committee.**

74 Decisions and Penalties

74.1 FINDING OF FACTS

The **protest committee** shall determine the facts and base its decision upon them. The finding of facts shall not be subject to appeal.

74.2 CONSIDERATION OF REDRESS

(a) When consideration of redress has been initiated as provided in rule 69, Requests for Redress, or rule 70.3, Yacht Materially Prejudiced, the **protest committee** shall decide whether the finishing position of a yacht or yachts has been materially prejudiced in any of the circumstances set out in rule 69.

(b) If so, the **protest committee** shall satisfy itself by taking appropriate evidence, especially before *abandoning* or *cancelling* the race, that it is aware of the relevant facts and of the probable consequences of any arrangement, to all yachts concerned for that particular race and for the series, if any, as a whole.

(c) The **protest committee** shall then make as equitable arrangement as possible for all yachts concerned. This may be to let the results of the race stand, to adjust the points score or the finishing time of the prejudiced yacht, to *abandon* or *cancel* the race or to adopt some other means.

74.3 MEASUREMENT PROTESTS

(a) A **protest** under rule 19, Measurement or Rating Certificates, or class rules that a measurement, scantling or flotation rule has been infringed while *racing*, or that a classification or rating certificate is invalid, may be decided by the **protest committee** immediately after the hearing, provided that it is satisfied there is no reasonable doubt as to the interpretation or application of the rules. When the **protest committee** is not so satisfied, it shall refer the question, together with the facts found, to an authority qualified to resolve such questions. The **protest committee,** in making its decision, shall be governed by the report of the authority.

(b) In addition to the requirements of rule 74.6, the body that issued the certificate of the yacht concerned shall also be notified.

(c) When an appeal under rule 77, Right of Appeal and Decisions, is lodged, the yacht may compete in further races, but subject to the results of that appeal.

74.4 PENALTIES AND EXONERATION

When the **protest committee** after finding the facts, or the race committee or **protest committee** acting under rule 70.1, Action by Race or Protest Committee, decides that:

(a) a yacht has infringed any of the **rules,** or

(b) in consequence of her neglect of any of the **rules,** a yacht has compelled other yachts to infringe any of the **rules,**

she shall be disqualified, unless the sailing instructions applicable to that race provide some other penalty, and, in the case of (b), the other yachts shall be exonerated. Such disqualification or other penalty shall be imposed irrespective of whether the **rule** that led to the disqualification or penalty was mentioned in the **protest,** or the yacht that was at fault was mentioned or protested, e.g., the protesting yacht or a third yacht may be disqualified and the protested yacht exonerated.

74.5 POINTS AND PLACES

(a) When a yacht either is disqualified or has retired after *finishing,* the following yachts shall each be moved up one place.

(b) When a yacht is penalised by being removed from a series or a part of a series, no races are to be re-scored and no changes are to be made in the scores of other yachts, except that, when the incident from which the penalty resulted occurred in a particular race, she shall be disqualified from that race and the yachts *finishing* behind her in that race shall each be moved up one place.

(c) When a scoring system provides that one or more scores are to be excluded in calculating a yacht's total score, a disqualification under Fundamental Rule C, Fair Sailing, Fundamental Rule D, Accepting Penalties, or rule 54, Propulsion, shall not be excluded.

74.6 THE DECISION

(a) After making its decision, the **protest committee** shall promptly communicate the following to the **parties to the protest:**

(i) the facts found,

(ii) the **rule** or **rules** judged applicable,

(iii) the decision and grounds on which it is based,

(iv)   the yacht or yachts penalised, if any, and

(v)   the penalty imposed, if any, or the redress granted, if any.

(b) A **party to the protest** shall on request be supplied with:

(i)   the above details in writing, and

(ii)   unless irrelevant, a diagram of the incident endorsed by the **protest committee.**

SECTION C—Special Rules

75   Gross Infringement of Rules or Misconduct

75.1 PENALTIES BY THE RACE COMMITTEE OR PROTEST COMMITTEE

(a) The race committee or **protest committee** may call a hearing when it has reasonable grounds for believing that a competitor has committed a gross infringement of the **rules** or a gross breach of good manners or sportsmanship.

(b) When the **protest committee** finds that there has been a gross infringement of the **rules** or a gross breach of good manners or sportsmanship, it may exclude a competitor, and a yacht when appropriate, either from further participation in a series, or from the whole series, or take other disciplinary action. The committee shall report any penalty imposed to its national authority, and to that of the competitor, and to that of the yacht.

(c) No action shall be taken under this rule without a written statement of allegation and a hearing held in accordance with the rules of Section B, Protest Procedure.

(d) Any hearing under this rule shall be conducted by a **protest committee** consisting of at least three members.

75.2 PENALTIES BY THE NATIONAL AUTHORITY
Upon a receipt of a report of gross infringement of the **rules** or a gross breach of good manners or sportsmanship, or a report of a penalty imposed under rule 75.1, a national authority may conduct an investigation and, when appropriate, a hearing and take such action as it deems appropriate against the person or persons or the yacht involved. Such action may include disqualification from participating in any race held in its jurisdiction for any period, or other disciplinary action. The national authority shall report any penalty imposed to the national authority of the competitor, and to that of the yacht, and to the International Yacht Racing Union. The IYRU shall inform all national authorities, which may also apply a penalty.

76   Liability

76.1 DAMAGES
The question of damages arising from an infringement of any of the **rules** shall be governed by the prescriptions, if any, of the national authority.

76.2 MEASUREMENT EXPENSES
Unless otherwise prescribed by the **protest committee,** the fees and expenses entailed by a **protest** on measurement or classification shall be paid by the unsuccessful party.

SECTION D—Appeals

77   Right of Appeal and Decisions

77.1 RIGHT OF APPEAL
Except when the right of appeal has been denied in accordance with rule 1.5(a) or (b), Right of Appeal, a **party to a protest** may appeal a decision of a **protest committee** to the national authority concerned. A race committee that is a **party to a protest** may appeal only the decision of an independent protest committee or jury.

77.2 RIGHT OF REFERENCE
A **protest committee** may refer its own decision to the national authority for confirmation or correction of its interpretation of the **rules.** A reference shall contain the **protest committee's** decision and the relevant documents listed in rule 78.1(b), (Appellant's Responsibilities).

77.3 QUESTIONS OF INTERPRETATION
When no **protest** that may be appealed is involved, a national authority may answer questions from a club or other organisation affiliated to it. A question shall contain sufficient detail for an interpretation to be made.

77.4 INTERPRETATION OF RULES
Appeals, references and questions shall be made only on interpretations of the **rules.** The national authority shall accept the **protest committee's** finding of facts, except that, when it is not satisfied with the facts presented, it may request further information from the **protest committee** or return the **protest** for a re-hearing.

77.5 INTERESTED PARTIES
No **interested party** or member of the **protest committee** shall take any part in the discussion or decision upon an appeal or reference.

77.6 DECISIONS

(a) A national authority may uphold, reverse or alter a **protest committee's** decision. When, from the facts found by the **protest committee**, it believes that any yacht that was a **party to the protest** infringed a **rule,** it shall penalise her, irrespective of whether that yacht or that **rule** was mentioned in the decision.

(b) The decision of the national authority shall be final, and shall be transmitted in writing by the national authority to all **parties to the protest** and the **protest committee,** who shall be bound by the decision.

78 Appeal Procedures

78.1 APPELLANT'S RESPONSIBILITIES

(a) Within 15 days of receiving the **protest committee's** written decision or its decision not to re-open a hearing, the appellant shall transmit to the national authority the dated appeal, which shall include the grounds for the appeal, i.e. why the appellant believes the **protest committee's** interpretation of the **rules** to be incorrect, and a copy of the **protest committee's** decision.

(b) Any of the following documents in the appellant's possession shall be sent with the appeal or as soon as possible thereafter:

   (i) the protest form(s);

   (ii) a diagram, prepared or endorsed by the **protest committee**, showing the force and direction of the wind; the set and rate of the current or tidal stream, if any; the course to the next *mark*, or the *mark* itself, and the required side; the positions and tracks of all yachts involved; and, if relevant, the depth of the water;

   (iii) the notice of race, the sailing instructions, any other conditions governing the *event*, and any amendments thereto;

   (iv) any written statements submitted by the **parties to the protest** to the **protest committee**;

   (v) any additional relevant documents; and

   (vi) the names and addresses of all **parties to the protest** and the protest committee chairman.

78.2 NOTIFICATION OF THE PROTEST COMMITTEE

Upon receipt of a valid appeal, the national authority shall transmit a copy of the appeal to the **protest committee,** informing the **protest committee** of the documents supplied by the appellant.

78.3 PROTEST COMMITTEE'S RESPONSIBILITIES

The **protest committee** shall transmit to the national authority the documents listed in rule 78.1(b) that were not supplied by the appellant. The **protest committee** shall include any comments on the appeal that it may wish to make.

78.4 NATIONAL AUTHORITY'S RESPONSIBILITIES

The national authority shall transmit copies of the appeal and any other relevant documents to the other **parties to the protest.** It shall transmit to the appellant copies of documents that were not supplied by the appellant.

78.5 COMMENTS

All **parties to the protest** may submit comments on the appeal to the national authority within a reasonable time, and at the same time shall transmit copies of such documents to the other **parties to the protest** and the **protest committee**.

78.6 FEE

A national authority may prescribe that a fee be paid for it to consider an appeal, reference or question, and shall allow a reasonable time for payment.

78.7 WITHDRAWING AN APPEAL

An appellant may withdraw an appeal by accepting the decision of the **protest committee**.

APPENDIX 1—Definition of an Amateur and Eligibility Regulations

1   Amateur

1.1   For the purpose of international yacht races in which yachts are required to have one or more amateurs on board and in other races with similar requirements, an amateur is a yachtsman who engages in yacht racing as a pastime as distinguished from a means of obtaining a livelihood or part-time compensation other than that permitted by the Guidelines to the Eligibility Code. No yachtsman shall lose amateur status by reason of his livelihood being derived from designing or constructing yachts, yacht parts, sails or accessories; or from similar professions associated with the sport; or solely from the maintenance (but not the *racing*) of yachts.

1.2   Competing in a race in which a prize is offered having a value greater than US$300, other than a prize awarded only for temporary possession, is ground for loss of amateur status unless prior to the event:

      (i)   the competitor assigns to the IYRU, his national authority or his national Olympic committee all his rights to such prize, or

      (ii)   the organising authority obtains its national authority's consent to a prize having a value greater than US$300.

1.3   Any yachtsman whose amateur status is questioned or is in doubt may apply to his national authority for recognition of his amateur status. Any such applicant may be required to provide such particulars and evidence and to pay such fees as the national authority may prescribe. Recognition may be suspended or cancelled by the national authority granting it, and, upon application by the competitor affected, the authority may reinstate recognition of amateur status following a period of at least two years absence from the sport.

1.4   The Permanent Committee of the IYRU or any tribunal nominated by the chairman of that committee may review the decision of any national authority affecting the amateur status of a yachtsman for the purpose of competing in international races.

2   I.O.C. Rule 26 - Eligibility Code

To be eligible for participation in the Olympic Games, a competitor must:

    —   observe and abide by the Rules of the International Olympic Committee (IOC) and in addition the rules of his or her International Federation (IF), as approved by the IOC, even if the Federation's rules are more strict than those of the IOC;

> — not have received any financial rewards or material benefit in connection with his or her sports participation, except as permitted in the bye-laws to this rule.

BYE-LAWS TO RULE 26

A. Each IF is responsible for the wording of the eligibility code relating to its sport, which must be approved by the Executive Board in the name of the IOC.

B. The observation of Rule 26 and of the eligibility codes of IFs are under the responsibility of IFs and National Olympic Committee (NOC) involved. The Eligibility Commission of the IOC will ensure the application of these provisions.

C. All cases of infringement of Rule 26 of the IOC and of the eligibility codes of IFs shall be communicated by the respective IF or NOC to the IOC to be taken in consideration by its eligibility commission. In accordance with Rule 23 and its bye-law, the accused competitor may request to be heard by the Executive Board whose decision will be final.

GUIDELINES TO ELIGIBILITY CODE FOR THE IFs

A. The following regulations are based on the principle that an athlete's health must not suffer nor must he or she be placed at a social or material disadvantage as a result of his or her preparation for and participation in the Olympic Games and international sports competitions. In accordance with Rule 26, the IOC, the IFs, the NOCs, and the National Authorities will assume responsibility for the protection and support of athletes.

B. All competitors, men or women, who conform to the criteria set out in Rule 26, may participate in the Olympic Games, except those who have:

1. been registered as professional athletes or professional coaches in any sport. Each National Authority shall provide a means for registering professional yachtsmen and women, and professional coaches. In this connection:

    (a) Professional yachtsmen or women shall be persons who do not comply with the definition of an amateur as defined in Appendix 1 of the current Yacht Racing Rules.

    (b) Professional coaches shall be persons who obtain their principal means of livelihood from teaching the skills of yacht racing.

2. signed a contract as a professional athlete or professional coach in any sport before the official closing of the Olympic Games.

3. accepted without the knowledge of their IF, National Authority or NOC a material advantage for their preparation or participation in yachting competition except:

(a)   either from, or with the permission of their National Authority; or

(b)   from funds held by the National Authority however obtained which are being held by that Authority or Trust for or on behalf of either an individual or class of yachtsmen.

(c)   National Authorities may issue guidelines for the receipt of such material advantages which shall cover:

      (i)   Reimbursement of expenses properly incurred in preparation for, and competing in an international or Olympic event.

      (ii)   The provision of equipment for such events.

      (iii)   Living and accommodation allowances and including allowances in lieu of normal salary, etc., if the same is lost due to the yachtsman engaging in such preparation or competition.

(d)   The receipt of money as a prize, or otherwise, not exceeding US$300 shall not be a breach of this clause.

4.   allowed their person, name, picture, or sports performances to be used for advertising, except when their IF, NOC or National Authority has entered into a contract for sponsorship or equipment. All payment must be made to the IF, NOC or National Authority concerned, and not to the athlete.

5.   carried advertising material on their person or clothing in the Olympic Games and Games under the patronage of the IOC, other than trademarks on technical equipment or clothing as agreed by the IOC with the IFs.

In the absence of any special agreement by the IOC with the IF's, advertising material on clothing shall not exceed that on clothing commercially available to the public *provided however* that only one maker's mark may be displayed on clothing worn by yachtsmen and provided that such a mark shall fit within a square not exceeding 100mm by 100mm.

6.   in the practice of sport and in the opinion of the IOC, manifestly contravened the spirit of fair play in the exercise of sport, particularly by the use of doping or violence.

APPENDIX 2—Sailboard Racing Rules

Sailboard races shall be *sailed* under the International Yacht Racing Rules modified as follows:

1   Part I - Definitions

1.1   *Leeward and Windward* - The *windward* side of a sailboard is the side that is, or, when head to wind or with the wind astern, was, towards the wind, regardless of the direction in which the sailboard is *sailing*. However, when *sailing* by the lee (i.e. with the wind coming over her stern from the stern from the same side as her boom is on) the *windward* side is the other side. The opposite side is the *leeward* side.

When neither of two sailboards on the same *tack* is *clear astern*, the one on the *windward* side of the other is the *windward sailboard*. The other is the *leeward sailboard*.

1.2   *Capsized* and *Recovering*

    (a)   *Capsized*—A sailboard is *capsized* when she is not under way due to her sail being is the water or when the competitor is waterstarting.

    (b)   *Recovering*—A sailboard is *recovering* from a *capsize* from the time her sail or, when waterstarting, the competitor's body is raised out of the water until she has steerage way.

2   Part III - General Requirements

2.1   Rule 19.1 - Measurement or Rating Certificates

When so prescribed by the national authority, a numbered and dated device on the board, daggerboard and sail shall rank as a measurement certificate.

2.2   Rule 23 - Anchor

An anchor and chain or rope need not be carried.

2.3   Rule 24 - Life Saving Equipment

A safety device shall prevent the mast separating from the board.

2.4   Rule 25 - Class Insignia, National Letters and Sail Numbers

Rule 25.1(a) - The class insignia shall be displayed once on each side of the sail. It shall fit within a rectangle of 0.5 m², the longer dimension of which shall not exceed one metre. It shall not refer to anything other than the manufacturer or class and shall not consist of more than two letters and three numbers. When approved by the IYRU or a national authority within its jurisdiction, this insignia shall not be considered to be advertising.

3   Part IV - Right of Way Rules

3.1   Rule 33 - Contact between Yachts Racing

As between each other, rule 33 shall not apply to sailboards.

3.2   Rule 38.2(a) - Proper Course Limitations
Rule 40 - Same Tack - Luffing before Clearing the Starting Line

For "mainmast" read "foot of mast".

3.3   Rule 46 - Person Overboard; Yacht Anchored; Aground or Capsized

Rule 46.3 does not apply.

3.4   Recovering from a Capsize

A sailboard *recovering* from a *capsize* shall not obstruct a sailboard or yacht under way.

3.5   Sail out of the Water when Starting

When approaching the starting line to *start*, a sailboard shall have her sail out of the water and in a normal position, except when *capsized* unintentionally.

3.6   Sailing Backward when Starting

When approaching the starting line to *start* or when on the course side of the starting line, a sailboard *sailing* or drifting backward shall keep clear of other sailboards and yachts.

4   Part V - Other Sailing Rules

Rule 54 - Propulsion

Dragging a foot in the water to check way is permissible. In rule 54.3(b), for "sheet" read "wishbone", and delete the last sentence.

5   Part VI - Protests, Penalties and Appeals

Rule 68 - Protests by Yachts

A sailboard need not display a flag in order to signify her intention to protest as required by rule 68.3, but, except when rule 68.4 applies, she shall try to notify the other sailboard or yacht by hail at the first reasonable opportunity and the race committee as soon as possible after *finishing* or retiring.

6   APPENDIX 3 - Alternative Penalties for Infringement of a Rule of Part IV

6.1   720° Turns

Unless otherwise prescribed in the sailing instructions, the 720° Turns penalty in Appendix 3.1 shall apply. Two full 360° turns of the board shall satisfy the provision of the 720° Turns penalty.

.2 Percentage

A sailboard need not display Code flag "I" to acknowledge an infringement. She shall notify the other sailboard or yacht by hail immediately and the race committee as soon as possible after *finishing* or retiring.

Rules for Multi-Mast Sailboards

.1 Part IV - Rule 38.2(a) and Rule 40

The normal station of the helmsman is the normal station of the crew member controlling the mainsail. The mainsail is the foremost sail and the mainmast is the foremost mast.

.2 Appendix 2 - Rule 1.2(a) *Capsized*

A multi-mast sailboard is *capsized* when one or more of her sails are in the water or one or more competitors are waterstarting.

.3 Appendix 2 - Rule 1.2(b) *Recovering*

A multi-mast sailboard is *recovering* from a *capsize* from the time her sails or, when waterstarting, the competitors' bodies are raised out of the water until she has steerage way.

3 Appendix 2 - Rule 3.4 - Sail out of the Water when Starting

For "sail" read "sails".

unboard Racing Rules

ese rules apply for alternative sailboard races only, i.e. course races and slalom, t not for triangle (Olympic course) races. Funboard races, both course races d slalom, shall be *sailed* under the International Yacht Racing Rules, Appendix modified as follows:

The following rules apply for both Course Races and Slalom.

Part V - Other Sailing Rules

1 Rule 52 - Touching a Mark

Rules 52.1(a)(ii) and (iii) do not apply.

2 Rule 54 - Propulsion

Rule 54 is replaced by: "A sailboard shall be propelled by the action of the wind on the sail, by the action of the water on the hull and by the unassisted actions of the competitor."

9 Part VI - Protests, Penalties and Appeals

9.1 Rule 68 - Protests by Yachts

A **protest** does not need to be in writing but may be made orally.

9.2 Rule 77 - Right of Appeal and Decisions

Except for a competitor or sailboard penalised under rule 75.1, Gross Infringement of Rules or Misconduct, the right of appeal is denied.

B. The following rules apply for Slalom only.

10 Part I - Definitions

10.1 *Going Out* and *Coming In* - when *sailing* from the shore against the incoming surf, a sailboard is *going out*. A sailboard *sailing* in the opposite direction is *coming in*.

10.2 *Overtaking* - A sailboard is *overtaking* from the moment she establishes an *overlap* from *clear astern* until she is *clear ahead* of the overtaken sailboard. When an *overlap* exists at the preparatory signal, the *windward sailboard* shall be deemed to be overtaking.

11 Part II - Organisation and Management

Rule 6 - Starting and Finishing Lines

The starting and finishing lines may be positioned on the shore.

12 Part IV - Right of Way Rules

12.1 Except for rule 37.2, rules 36 to 42 do not apply.

12.2 Basic Rules

    (a) A sailboard *coming in* shall keep clear of a sailboard *going out*.

    (b) When neither *going out* nor *coming in*, a *port-tack* sailboard shall keep clear of a *starboard-tack* sailboard.

12.3 Changing Tacks - Tacking and Gybing

Except when *gybing* around a *mark*, a sailboard that is *tacking* or *gybing* shall keep clear of a sailboard *on a tack*.

12.4 Same Tack - Overtaking

An *overtaking* sailboard shall keep clear of the overtaken sailboard.

APPENDIX 3 - Alternative Penalties for Infringement of a Rule of Part IV

Experience indicates that the 720° turns penalty is most satisfactory for small boats in relatively short races, but that it can be dangerous for large yachts and in restricted waters and not sufficiently severe in long races. The 20% penalty is relatively mild and is designed to encourage acknowledgement of infringements and willingness to protest when not acknowledged. Both systems keep yachts *racing*.

Either of the following alternatives to disqualification may be used by including in the sailing instructions a provision such as the following (or if preferred the selected penalty may be quoted in full):

"The 720° Turns penalty, Appendix 3.1 (or the Percentage penalty, Appendix 3.2) of the racing rules will apply."

720° Turns

1 A yacht that may have infringed a rule of Part IV may accept an alternative penalty by *sailing* well clear of all other yachts as soon as possible after the incident, and remaining clear while she makes two complete 360° turns (720°) in the same direction, including two *tacks* and two *gybes*.

2 When the infringement occurs at the finishing line, she shall make her turns on the course side of the line before she will be recorded as having *finished*.

3 A yacht intending to protest shall hail the other yacht immediately and act in accordance with rule 68, Protests by Yachts. A yacht that accepts an alternative penalty may protest with respect to the same incident. She shall not be penalised further for an infringement for which she accepted the penalty, except as provided by paragraph 1.4.

4 The **protest committee** may disqualify a yacht that has accepted an alternative penalty when it finds that her infringement resulted in serious damage or that she gained a significant advantage.

5 Failure to accept an alternative penalty will make an infringing yacht liable to disqualification or other prescribed penalty. When a yacht complies with some but not all of the requirements of paragraphs 1.1 or 1.2, the yacht infringed against is relieved of further obligations under rule 33, Contact between Yachts Racing.

Percentage

1 A yacht that may have infringed a rule of Part IV may accept an alternative penalty:

(a) by displaying Code flag "I" at the first reasonable opportunity after the incident, and

155

(b)   except for a yacht *sailed* single-handed, by keeping it displayed until she has *finished*, and

(c)   by reporting her acknowledgement and the yacht infringed against to the race committee immediately after *finishing*.

She shall receive a score for the place worse than her actual finishing position by 20% of the number of starters*, but not less than three places, calculated in accordance with paragraph 2.7.

2.2   A yacht intending to protest shall hail the other yacht immediately and act in accordance with rule 68, Protests by Yachts. A yacht that accepts an alternative penalty may protest with respect to the same incident; however her penalty shall not be affected. She shall not be penalised further for an infringement for which she accepted the penalty, except as provided by paragraph 2.5.

2.3   A yacht may protest without displaying a protest flag against a yacht that has complied with some but not all of the requirements of paragraph 2.1.

2.4   A yacht that does not comply with the requirements of paragraph 2.1, but acknowledges an infringement prior to a hearing, shall be penalised 50% but not less than six places.

2.5   The **protest committee** may disqualify a yacht that has accepted an alternative penalty when it finds that her infringement resulted in serious damage or that she gained a significant advantage.

2.6   Failure to accept an alternative penalty will make an infringing yacht liable to disqualification or other prescribed penalty. When a yacht complies with some but not all of the requirements of paragraph 2.1, the yacht infringed against is relieved of further obligations under rule 33, Contact between Yachts Racing. A yacht may request a hearing solely on the point of having complied with the requirements of paragraph 2.1.

2.7   The penalty shall be computed as 20% (or 50%) of the number of starters in the event to the nearest whole number (round .5 upward), such number to be not less than three (or six), except that a yacht shall not receive a score worse than for one position more than the number of starters* (Examples: an infringing yacht finishing 8th in a start for 19 yachts would receive a score for 12th place: 8 + (19 x 20% = 3.8 or 4) = 12. Another infringing yacht, finishing 18th, would receive the score for 20th place. The imposition of a percentage penalty shall not affect the scores of other yachts. Thus, two yachts may receive the same score.

2.8   A yacht infringing a rule in more than one incident shall receive a penalty for each incident.

* When scoring a regatta, these calculations shall be based on the number of yachts entered in the series, not the number of starters in the race in question.

APPENDIX 4—Team Racing and Match Racing Rules

SECTION A—Team Racing Rules

Team racing shall be *sailed* under the International Yacht Racing Rules supplemented and altered as follows:

1 Sailing Rules

1.1 Except when *sailing* a *proper course*, a yacht shall not act to interfere with another yacht *sailing* on a different leg of the course. Each time a leg is *sailed*, it is a different leg.

.2 Right of way may be waived between team-mate yachts, provided that doing so does not directly affect a yacht of the other team adversely.

.3 When contact occurs between team-mate yachts and neither promptly displays a green flag, rule 33, Contact between Yachts Racing, will apply, except that only the lower-scoring yacht shall receive the penalty points prescribed in paragraph 3.4(c). A yacht disabled by a team-mate yacht is ineligible for redress under rule 69(c), Requests for Redress.

.4 Except to protect her position or that of a team-mate yacht, a yacht that is *sailing* the last leg of the course shall not act to interfere with a yacht of another team that has no opponent astern of her. A team-mate yacht shall not attempt to render this rule inapplicable by reducing speed or departing from a *proper course*.

.5 Rule 41.3, Onus, does not apply.

.6 A yacht that receives assistance from a team-mate yacht does not infringe rule 60, Outside Assistance.

Acknowledgement of Infringements; Intention to Protest

.1 A yacht may acknowledge an infringement of a rule of Part IV, except rule 32, Serious Damage, by hailing such acknowledgement to the yacht infringed against immediately, and by promptly displaying a green flag. After displaying the flag, she shall not remove it. She shall display one green flag for each incident, unless all green flags supplied are already displayed.

.2 A yacht intending to protest shall hail the other yacht immediately and promptly display a red flag. She shall display one red flag for each incident, unless all red flags supplied are already displayed. A yacht that has displayed a red flag and that decides reasonably promptly thereafter that she, and not the other yacht, was at fault shall immediately replace the red flag with a green flag and hail the other yacht accordingly.

2.3 When a yacht displaying a red flag with respect to an incident is satisfied that the other yacht has displayed a green flag in accordance with paragraph 2.1 or 2.2, she shall immediately remove her red flag.

3 Scoring a Race

3.1 Each yacht *finishing* a race shall score three-quarters of a point for first place, two points for second place, three points for third place, and so on. A yacht that does not *start*, *finish* or *sail* the course shall receive points equal to the number of yachts entitled to *race*. Each yacht, including one that retires, shall also receive penalty points as provided in paragraph 3.4. The team with the lower total points wins.

3.2 When all yachts of one team have *finished* or retired, the race committee may stop the race. Other yachts still *racing* shall receive the points they would have scored had they *finished*.

3.3 When all the yachts of a team forfeit or fail to *start* in a race, each shall receive points equal to the number of yachts entitled to *race*, and the yachts of the other team shall be scored as if they had *finished* in the best positions.

3.4 In addition to the points prescribed above, a yacht shall receive penalty points as follows:

	Infringement	Penalty Points
(a)	An infringement of a rule of Part IV, other than rule 32, acknowledged in accordance with paragraph 2.1.	2.5
(b)	Failure to *start*, *finish* or *sail* the course.	2.5
(c)	An infringement of any **rule**, other than rule 32, not acknowledged in accordance with paragraph 2.1.	6
(d)	An infringement of rule 32.	10

When a yacht gains a significant advantage from an infringement of a rule of Part IV that was acknowledged in accordance with paragraph 2.1, she may be further penalised.

4 Scoring a Series

4.1 A team racing series shall consist of races or matches. A match shall consist of two races between the same two teams. The team with the lower total points for the race or the match shall be the winner.

4.2 When two or more teams are competing in a series consisting of races or matches, the series winner shall be the team winning the greatest number of races or matches. The other teams shall be ranked in order of number of wins. Tied matches shall count as one-half win to each team.

3   When there is a tie:

   (a)   Ties between two teams will be broken in favour of the winner of the match or race when the two teams met, or, failing this, the winner of the second race of that match.

   (b)   Ties between three or more teams will be broken in favour of the team or teams scoring the lowest aggregate points when the tied teams met, or, failing this, the lowest total points in the series. Failing this, the tie shall be broken by drawing lots.

When Organising Authorities Supply All Yachts

Assignment of Yachts

1   The organising authority shall form groups of yachts, and for the first race shall draw lots to assign the groups to the teams. The groups of yachts shall be exchanged between races so that, in so far as possible, each team uses each group the same number of times. The organising authority shall identify each yacht within her group by use of special sail numbers or by display of a distinctive colour in her rigging or on her hull or sails.

2   In a two-team series after an even number of races, either team may require that the yachts be re-grouped. The groups will be assigned for the next race by the spin of a coin, except that, when there will be a final odd race in a series between a host team and a visiting team, the visiting team shall choose the group it will use.

3   Sails and other equipment shall remain with a yacht throughout the event, except when damage or loss requires the race committee to make substitutions. In such case, it shall inform all teams affected thereby.

Breakdowns

1   A yacht suffering a breakdown shall display a red flag as soon as practicable and, when possible, continue *racing*.

2   When the race committee decides that the yacht's finishing position was materially prejudiced, that the breakdown was not the fault of the crew, and that in the circumstances a reasonably competent crew would not have been able to avoid the material prejudice, it shall make as equitable a decision as possible, which may be to order the race to be re-sailed, or, when the yacht's finishing position was predictable, award her points for that position. In case of doubt as to her position when she broke down, the doubt shall be resolved against her.

3   A breakdown caused by defective equipment, or by an infringement by an opponent, shall not normally be deemed to be the fault of the crew,

but one caused by careless handling, capsizing or by an infringement by a yacht of the same team shall be. When in doubt about the fault of the crew, the race committee shall resolve it in the yacht's favour.

SECTION B—Match Racing Rules

Match racing shall be *sailed* under the International Yacht Racing Rules as altered by this appendix. A match is a race between two yachts. The sailing instructions may prescribe that parts of the appendix will not apply or make further alterations in accordance with rule 3.1, Sailing Instructions.

1   Alterations to the Racing Rules

1.1   Rule 32 is altered to read: "A right-of-way yacht shall attempt to avoid collision resulting in damage."

1.2   Rule 39 is altered to read: "A yacht that is on a free leg of the course shall not *sail* below her *proper course* when she is clearly within three of her overall lengths of a *leeward yacht.*"

1.3   Rules 64.2 and 64.3 are altered to read: "A spinnaker may be set without a boom. When a spinnaker boom is used, it shall be carried only on the side of the mast opposite to the main boom and shall be fixed to the mast except when shifting it or the sail attached to it."

2   Further Alterations to the Rules when Umpiring (On-the-water judging) is used

2.1   Fundamental Rule D - Add: "A yacht may wait for the umpires' decision before taking a penalty."

2.2   Rule 33 does not apply.

2.3   Rule 38.2(c) is altered to read: "When there is doubt, the *leeward yacht* may assume that she has the right to *luff* or *sail* above her *proper course* unless the *windward yacht* has made an audible sound signal. The *leeward yacht* shall be governed by such a signal."

2.4   Rules 41.3, 42.1(c) and (d), and 43.2(b)(iii) do not apply.

2.5   In so far as the provisions of match racing rule 5 conflict with the rules of Part VI, Part VI does not apply.

3   Additional Right of Way Rules

3.1   A yacht shall not act to interfere with:

(a) a yacht on another leg of the course, or

(b) a yacht in another match, or

(c) a penalised yacht that is getting clear and while she is exonerating herself.

2   A yacht that is exonerating herself shall keep clear of the other yacht until she has completed her penalty and is on a *proper course* to the next *mark*.

3   When umpiring is being used, infringements of this rule will be signalled in accordance with rule 5.2(c).

Pre-Start Procedure

1   Before her preparatory signal, a yacht shall proceed to and remain outside the end of the starting line assigned to her.

2   Within the two-minute period following her preparatory signal, a yacht shall cross the starting line from the course side to the pre-start side, and shall keep clear of any yachts *racing* in a preceding match until she is wholly on the pre-start side.

3   Infringement of this rule is not open to protest by a yacht.

Umpiring, Protest Procedure, Penalties

1   UMPIRES
For a match racing event where decisions are to be made on the water, umpires who have an intimate knowledge of the **rules** and are experienced in judging match races shall be appointed. Umpires may serve on the jury appointed to hear **protests** arising under rule 5.5(e).

2   PROTESTS ALLEGING INFRINGEMENT OF A RIGHT OF WAY RULE
For **protests** alleging infringements of the rules of Sections B and C of Part IV, Sections A and B of Part VI are modified as follows:

(a) An umpires' vessel with at least two umpires aboard will be assigned to each match.

(b) When a yacht considers that the other yacht has infringed a rule of Sections B and C of Part IV, she may protest by immediately and conspicuously displaying Code flag "Y" from her backstay (or shroud when no backstay) and hailing "Protest".

(c) As soon as possible thereafter, the umpires will decide whether either or both yachts have infringed such a rule. The umpires will immediately inform both yachts of their decision by displaying a visual signal accompanied by a sound signal as follows:

    (i)   A green flag means: "No infringement";

      (ii)   A placard identifying a yacht means: "The designated yacht has infringed a rule, is penalised and shall exonerate herse in accordance with rule 5.2(e)".

(d)   The protesting yacht shall lower Code flag "Y" as soon as possibl after the umpires' signal.

(e)   Unless otherwise prescribed in the sailing instructions, the penalise yacht shall *sail* clear of the other yacht and do a 270° turn, includin a *gybe*. When the penalty is signalled:

      (i)   before the starting signal, it shall be done as soon as possibl after *starting*.

      (ii)   on a windward leg, it shall be done as soon as possible.

      (iii)   on a free leg, it shall be done as soon as possible afte commencing the next windward leg.

(f)   When the umpires fail to make a signal required by rule 5.2(c):

      (i)   a protested yacht may acknowledge the infringement by takin the penalty prescribed under rule 5.2(e);

      (ii)   when no penalty is taken with respect to that protest, th umpires may act in accordance with rule 5.5(b) or (e).

5.3   NON-ACCEPTABLE PROTESTS

A yacht shall not protest the other yacht for an alleged infringement of th rules of Section A of Part IV, or rule 52, Touching a Mark, or rule 5 Propulsion.

5.4   ACTION BY UMPIRES

When the umpires decide that a yacht:

(a)   has failed to comply with rule 5.2, or

(b)   has infringed rule 52, Touching a Mark, or rule 54, Propulsion,

(c)   has caused damage to either yacht, or

(d)   after completing her penalty, has gained an advantage over the oth yacht.

they may penalise the yacht in accordance with rules 5.2(c) and (e) disqualify the yacht and terminate the match. Such disqualification ar termination will be signalled by the display of a black flag with the placa designating the penalised yacht.

5.5   PROTESTS BASED ON OTHER RULES AND REQUESTS FC REDRESS

(a)   A yacht can protest another yacht for an alleged infringement of sailing instruction or a **rule** other than those specified in rules 5.2 ar

5.3, or can request redress in accordance with racing rule 69, Requests for Redress. Such a **protest** shall be signalled by displaying Code flag "B" or a rectangular red flag conspicuously from her backstay (or shroud if no backstay) until acknowledged by the umpires or the race committee.

(b) Following the race, the umpires will take testimony in any way they deem appropriate, and may make a decision that may be communicated orally.

(c) The umpires may act independently and may decide that a yacht has infringed a sailing instruction or **rule** other than those specified in rules 5.2 and 5.4, and may communicate the decision orally.

(d) When the umpires decide that a yacht has infringed a **rule** that has had no significant effect on the outcome of the match, a penalty of one-third of a point may be imposed.

(e) When the umpires deem it more appropriate to conduct a hearing ashore, or to re-open or resume a hearing held at sea, the yachts will be advised and a jury appointed that will proceed in accordance with the rules of Part VI.

.6 APPEALS
There shall be no appeals from decisions or re-opening of decisions made in accordance with rules 5.2 and 5.4.

Scoring

.1 Points are awarded to yachts, except that when yachts are interchanged, the points are awarded to helmsmen. The winner of each match scores one point, the loser scores no points. The winner is the one with the most points at the end of a series. When there is a round robin series (in which each races against all the others), and then a semi-final or final series, points from each series are not carried forward to the next.

.2 A yacht that has won a match but is disqualified for an infringement against a yacht in another match shall lose the point for that match. However, the losing yacht shall not be awarded the point.

.3 A two-way tie in a round robin series shall be decided by the result of the match between the tied yachts. When possible, this principle shall be applied when more than two are tied.

.4 When rule 6.3 does not resolve a tie, it shall, when practicable, be resolved by a sail-off or otherwise in a manner prescribed by the race committee.

APPENDIX 5—Scoring Systems

The two scoring systems most often used are the Olympic and the Low-Point. The Olympic system has been adopted for many class championships; the Low-Point system is suitable both for championships and for club and other small fleet racing, and is somewhat easier to use for race committees and competitors.

In both systems, lower points designate better finishing places. The Low-Point system uses a 'straight line' points schedule that rewards performance in direct proportion to finishing place; the Olympic system uses a "curved" points schedule that provides an additional reward in the top six finishing places. Although designed primarily for scoring regattas, either system may be used for other series; see paragraph 3, Suggested Alterations for Non-Regatta Series.

The sailing instructions may include a complete system verbatim or may incorporate either system by reference, with or without alterations, as explained in the notes following each system. See also Appendix 12, Sailing Instructions Guide, Instruction 18.

1 The Olympic Scoring System

1.1 NUMBER OF RACES, MINIMUM REQUIRED, AND RACES TO COUNT
There will be seven races, of which five shall be completed to constitute a series. Each yacht's total score will be the sum of her scores for all races excluding her worst score in accordance with rule 74.5(c), Points and Places. The lowest total score wins.

1.2 POINTS
Each yacht *finishing* in a race and not thereafter retiring or being disqualified will be scored points as follows:

Finishing Place	Points
First	0
Second	3
Third	5.7
Fourth	8
Fifth	10
Sixth	11.7
Seventh and thereafter	Place plus six

All other yachts, including a yacht that *finishes* and thereafter retires or is disqualified, will be scored points for the finishing place one more than the number of yachts entered in the series.

1.3 TIES
When there is a tie on total points between two or more yachts, the tie will be broken in favour of the yacht or yachts with the most first places and, when the tie remains, the most second places, and so on, if necessary.

for such races as count for total points. When the tie still remains, it shall stand as part of the final results.

Notes:
(a) The sailing instructions can incorporate the Olympic system by stating "The Olympic Scoring System, Appendix 5.1 of the racing rules, will apply."

(b) When the number of races is not seven, add "except that __ races are scheduled, of which __ shall be completed to constitute a series." (Insert the numbers of races.)

(c) When all races are to be counted, add "except that each yacht's total score will be the sum of her scores for all races."

2   The Low-Point Scoring System

2.1 NUMBER OF RACES, MINIMUM REQUIRED, AND RACES TO COUNT
The number of races scheduled and the number required to constitute a series shall be prescribed in the sailing instructions. Each yacht's total score will be the sum of her scores for all races, excluding her worst score in accordance with rule 74.5(c), Points and Places. The lowest total score wins.

2.2 POINTS
Each yacht *finishing* in a race and not thereafter retiring or being disqualified will be scored points equal to her finishing place, minus one-quarter point for first place, as follows:

Finishing Place	Points
First	3/4
Second	2
Third	3
Fourth	4
and so on.	

All other yachts, including a yacht that *finishes* and thereafter retires or is disqualified, will be scored points for the finishing place one more than the number of yachts entered in the series.

2.3 TIES
When there is a tie on total points between two or more yachts, the tie will be broken in favour of the yacht or yachts with the most first places, and, when the tie remains, the most second places, and so on, if necessary, for such races as count for total points. When the tie still remains, it shall stand as part of the final results.

Notes:
(d) The sailing instructions can incorporate the Low-Point system by stating "The Low-Point Scoring System, Appendix 5.2 of the racing rules, will apply, with __ races scheduled of which __ shall be completed to constitute a series." (Insert the numbers of races.)

(e)   When all races are to be counted, add "except that each yacht's total score will be the sum of her scores for all races."

3   Suggested Alterations for Non-Regatta Series

3.1   In a regatta all yachts are expected to compete in all races, and the difference between the number of entrants and the number of starters is usually insignificant. However, in a longer series there may be a number of yachts that compete in fewer races than others, in which case it is suggested that the following be substituted for the last paragraph in either 1.2 or 2.2:

> A yacht that does not *start* or rank as a starter in accordance with rule 50, Ranking as a Starter, will be scored points for the finishing place one more than the number of yachts entered in the series. All other yachts, including a yacht that *finishes* but thereafter retires or is disqualified, will be scored points for the finishing place one more than the number of yachts that *started* or ranked as starters in accordance with rule 50 in that race.

3.2   When it is desired to increase the number of races to be excluded from each yacht's series score, change the second sentence in 1.1 or 2.1 to read: "excluding her __ worst scores". (Insert the number.)

4   Guidance for Race and Protest Committees

4.1   ABBREVIATIONS FOR SCORING RECORDS
The following abbreviations are recommended to record the various occurrences that may determine a particular score:

DNC	Did not compete; i.e. did not *start* or rank as a starter under rule 50, Ranking as a Starter.
DNS	Did not *start*; i.e. ranked as a starter under rule 50 but failed to *start*.
PMS	Started prematurely or otherwise failed to comply with the starting procedure.
DNF	Did not *finish*.
RET	Retired after *finishing*.
DSQ	Disqualified.
DND	Disqualification not discardable under rule 74.5(c), Points and Places.
YMP	Yacht materially prejudiced.

4.2   REDRESS
In applying rule 74.2, Consideration of Redress, when it is deemed equitable to adjust the score of the prejudiced yacht by awarding points different from those she received for the race in question, the following possibilities are to be considered:

(i)   Points equal to the average, to the nearest tenth of a point (round .05 upward), of her points in all the races in the series except [her worst race and]* the race in question.

*Delete these words when all scores count for series results, or alter when more than one race is to be excluded.

(ii)   Points equal to the average, to the nearest tenth of a point (round .05 upward), of her points in all the races before the race in question.

(iii)   An arbitrary number of points based on the position of the yacht in the race in question at the time she was prejudiced.

APPENDIX 6—Recommended Protest Committee Procedure

In a protest hearing, the **protest committee** should give equal weight to all testimony; should recognize that honest testimony can vary and even be in conflict as a result of different observations and recollections; should resolve such differences as best it can; should recognize that no yacht is guilty until her infringement has been established to the satisfaction of the **protest committee;** should keep an open mind until all the evidence has been submitted as to whether the protestor or the protestee or a third yacht, when one is involved in the incident, has infringed a **rule.**

1   Preliminaries

1.1   Note on the **protest** the time at which it is received.

1.2   Determine whether the **protest** contains the information called for by rule 68.5, Particulars to be Included, in sufficient detail to identify the incident and the protested yacht, and to tell the recipient what the **protest** is about. If not, ask the protestor to supply the information (rule 68.8, Remedying Defects in the Protest). When a **protest** by a yacht does not identify the nature of the incident, it shall be refused (rules 68.8(a) and 73.2, Acceptance or Refusal of a Protest).

1.3   Unless the **protest** already provides the information;

Inquire whether the protestor displayed a protest flag in accordance with rule 68.3, unless rule 68.4 applies or the protestor is seeking redress under rule 69, and note his answer on the **protest.** When a protest flag has not been properly displayed, the **protest** shall be refused; rule 73.2, Acceptance or Refusal of a Protest, refers, except when the **protest committee** decides either:

(a)   rule 68.4 applies; or

(b)   it was impossible for the yacht to have displayed a protest flag, because she was, for example, dismasted, capsized or sunk.

1.4   Unless the **protest** already provides the information;

Inquire whether the protestor tried to inform the protested yacht(s) (the protestee(s)) that a **protest** would be lodged (rule 68.2, Informing the Protested Yacht) and note his answer on the **protest.** Rule 68.2 is mandatory with regard to the attempt to inform, but not with regard to its success.

See that the protest fee, if any, required by the sailing instructions is included and note its receipt on the **protest** (rule 68.7, Fee).

1.5   When the **protest** conforms to the requirements of rule 68, arrange to hold a hearing as soon as possible. Notify the representative of each yacht involved of the time and place of the hearing (rule 72, Notification of Parties).

1.6 The **protest** and any written statement regarding the incident (preferably photocopies) shall be available to all **parties to the protest** and to the **protest committee** for study before the taking of evidence. A reasonable time shall be allowed for the preparation of defence (rule 72, Notification of Parties).

2 The Hearing

2.1 The **protest committee** shall ensure that:

(a) a quorum is present as required by the organising authority. The quorum is not affected when it is considered desirable that some members of the **protest committee** leave the hearing during the discussion and decision.

(b) no **interested party** is a member of the **protest committee** or takes part in the discussion or decision. Ask the **parties to the protest** whether they object to any member on the grounds of "interest". Such an objection shall be made before the **protest** is heard (rule 71.2, Interested Parties).

(c) when any member of the **protest committee** saw the incident, he shall only give his evidence as a witness in the presence of the **parties to the protest** and may be questioned (rule 73.4, Evidence of Committee Member).

(d) when a hearing concerns a request for redress under rule 69, Requests for Redress, or rule 70.3, Yacht Materially Prejudiced, involving a member of the race committee, it is desirable that he is not a member of the **protest committee** and would therefore appear only as a witness.

2.2 The **parties to the protest** or a representative of each (with a language interpreter, when needed) shall have the right to be present throughout the hearing. Each witness, unless he is a member of the **protest committee,** shall be excluded, except when giving his evidence. Others may be admitted as observers at the discretion of the **protest committee** (rule 73.1, Right to be Present).

2.3 Invite first the protestor and then the protestee(s) to give their accounts of the incident. Each may question the other(s). Questions by the **protest committee,** except for clarifying details, are preferably deferred until all accounts have been presented. Models are useful. Positions before and after the incident itself are often helpful.

2.4 Invite the protestor and then the protestee to call witnesses. They may be questioned by the protestor and protestee as well as by the **protest committee.** The **protest committee** may also call witnesses. It may be appropriate and prudent to ask a witness to disclose any business or other relationship through which he might have an interest or might stand to benefit from the outcome of the **protest.**

2.5 Invite first the protestor and then the protestee to make a final statement of his case, including any application or interpretation of the **rules** to the incident as he sees it.

2.6 The **protest committee** may adjourn a hearing in order to obtain additional evidence.

3 Decision

3.1 The **protest committee,** after dismissing those involved in the incident, shall decide what the relevant facts are (rule 74.1, Finding of Facts).

3.2 The **protest committee** shall then apply the **rules** and reach a decision as to who, if anyone, infringed a **rule** and what **rule** was infringed (rule 74, Decisions and Penalties).

3.3 Having reached a decision in writing, recall the protestor and the protestee and read to them the facts found, the decision and the grounds for it (rule 74.6).

3.4 Any **party to the protest** is entitled to a copy of the decision (rule 74.6), signed by the chairman of the **protest committee.** A copy should also be filed with the committee records.

APPENDIX 10—Weighing of Wet Clothing (Racing Rule 61)

To test the weight of clothing and equipment worn by a competitor all items to be weighed shall be taken off and thoroughly soaked in water. Note: Equipment includes items such as trapeze harness, life jacket and heavy jacket.

The manner in which the clothing and equipment is arranged on the rack has a considerable effect on the weight recorded, and it is important that free draining is achieved without the formation of pools of water in the clothing. It is recommended that a rack comprised of "clothes hanger" type bars be used and that provision is made for suspending boots or shoes in an inverted position.

Pockets in clothing that are designed to be self-draining - i.e. those that have drain holes and no provision for closing them - shall be empty during the weighing; however, pockets or equipment designed to hold water as ballast shall be full when weighing takes place. Boots and shoes shall be empty when weighed.

Ordinary clothing becomes saturated within a few seconds but "heavy jackets" of the water absorbent type require longer and should be immersed for not less than two minutes.

On removal from the water the items shall be allowed to drain freely for one minute, at the end of which period the weight shall be recorded.

When the weight recorded exceeds the amount permitted, the measurer may allow the competitor to repeat the test twice by rearranging the clothing and equipment on the rack, re-soaking and re-weighing. When a lesser weight results, that weight shall be taken as the actual weight of clothing and equipment.

APPENDIX 12—Sailing Instructions Guide

This guide provides a set of checked and tested instructions that may be used verbatim for any regatta that will be sailed on a single course. Thus they will be particularly useful for most world, continental, national and other principal events. Also, when a regatta will use more than one course, the sailing instruction regarding courses can be altered appropriately; and most, if not all, other instructions will be applicable as they stand.

Some instructions are required or strongly recommended, while others are optional. Those that are required or recommended are shown with an asterisk (*).

The principles on which all sailing instructions should be based are as follows:

1 They should include only two types of statement: the intentions of the race committee and the obligations of competitors.

2 They should be concerned only with racing. Other information should be communicated through other means. For example: measurement regulations, requirements concerning registration of competitors or yachts, assignment of moorings, liability insurance, etc. should be in different documents.

3 They should not alter the racing rules, unless it is clearly desirable.

4 They should not repeat or restate any of the racing rules.

5 They should not repeat themselves.

6 The order of the instructions should reflect the chronological order in which the competitor will use them.

7 When possible, words or phrases used in the racing rules should be used in writing sailing instructions.

To use the guide in the preparation of sailing instructions, first delete all optional instructions that will not be needed. Then, following the instructions in the left margin, fill in the required information and select the alternatives desired. Finally, re-number all instructions in sequential order.

NOTE: The notes in this column contain guidance for preparing sailing instructions. Do not include them in the completed draft.

Insert: The full name of the regatta. The inclusive dates from measurement or the practice race until the final race. The name of the organising authority. The city and the country.

_____

_____

_____

_____

Sailing Instructions

*1. Rules

Insert the full names of the national authority when applicable, and the class(es).
Insert the appropriate category in accordance with Appendix 14.

The regatta will be governed by the International Yacht Racing Rules, the prescriptions of the ● , the rules of the ● class(es), (except as any of these are altered by these sailing instructions) and by these sailing instructions. The regatta is classified as a Category ● event.

*2 Entries

Eligible yachts may be entered by completing registration with the organising authority.

*3 Notices to Competitors

Insert the specific location(s).

Notices to competitors will be posted on the official notice board(s) located ● .

*4 Changes in Sailing Instructions

Insert the times.

Any change in the sailing instructions will be posted before ● on the day it will take effect, except that any change in the schedule of races will be posted by ● on the day before it will take effect.

5 Signals Made Ashore

Insert the specific location.

5.1 Signals made ashore will be displayed at ● .

*Insert the sound signal
and time.*

5.2 Code flag "AP", Answering Pendant, with two ● , (one ● when lowered) means "The race is postponed. The warning signal will be made not less than ● minutes after "AP" is lowered".

Insert the sound signal.

5.3 Code flag "B" at "the dip" with one ● means "Protest time has begun". When fully hoisted it means "There are less than 30 minutes remaining before protest time ends". When lowered it means "Protest time has ended".

*6 Schedule of Races

*Insert the days, dates
and times.*

Races are scheduled as follows:

Race   Day and Date   Time of Warning Signal

7 Class Flags

*Insert the class names
and descriptions of flags.
Use only for a multi-class
regatta.*

Class flags will be:

Class   Flag

8 Racing Area

*A section of a chart or
other suitable map should
be copied and marked
for this purpose.*

The racing area will be as shown in illustration "A", attached.

9 The Course

*Insert the distances.
Delete the last sentence
when not applicable.*

*9.1 The diagram below shows the course, including the approximate angles between legs, the order in which marks are to be rounded or passed, and the side on which each mark is to be left. Mark 1 will be approximately ● nautical miles from Mark 3. The first and last legs will be approximately ● longer than the distance from Mark 3 to Mark 1.

Insert course diagram(s) here. A method of illustrating a course is shown in Appendix A, Illustrating the Course. When there are navigational marks that are to be observed, they should be shown on the course chart.

9.2 The approximate compass bearing from the starting line to Mark 1 will be displayed from the race committee signal boat.

9.3 Courses will not be shortened.

*10   Marks

Insert the description of the marks and the instruction number.

Marks 1, 2 and 3 will be   ●   . New marks, when used in accordance with instruction ● , Change of Course after the Start, will be   ● . The starting and finishing marks will be   ● .

11   The Start

Use the last part of the sentence for a multi-class regatta. Insert the number of minutes.

*11.1 Races will be started in accordance with racing rule 4.4(a) System 1, with classes starting at ● minute intervals in the order ● .

(OR)

*11.1 Races will be started in accordance with racing rule 4.4(a) System 2, with classes starting at ● minute intervals in the order ● .

*11.2 The starting line will be between a staff displaying an orange flag or shape on the race committee boat at the starboard end and Mark 3 at the port end.

(OR)

*11.2 The starting line will be between a staff displaying an orange flag or shape on the race committee boat at the starboard end and the port end starting mark.

(OR)

Delete the last sentence when signals will be made from the starboard end race committee boat.

*11.2 The starting line will be between staffs displaying orange flags or shapes on two race committee boats. Signals will be made from a race committee signal boat stationed to windward of the line.

(OR)

*11.2 (a) The starting line will between staffs displaying orange flags on Starting Marks A and B and between staffs displaying orange flags on Starting Marks B and C as shown below. Mark B may not be on a straight line between Mark A and Mark C.

Mark A ●   ●   ● Mark C
Mark B

(b) For the purpose of racing rules 51.1(b) and 51.1(c), the extensions of the starting line are the extensions beyond Mark A and Mark C.

(c) When a yacht both touches Mark B and infringes racing rule 51.1(c), she may

175

exonerate herself by completing one rounding of either Mark A or Mark C.

Use only for a multi-class regatta. Insert "warning" when classes start at ten-minute intervals, "preparatory" when they start at five-minute intervals.

11.3 Yachts whose ● signal has not been made shall keep clear of the starting area and of all yachts whose ● signal has been made.

Insert the number of minutes.

11.4 A yacht shall not start later than ● minutes after her starting signal.

12 Recalls

Insert "in accordance with racing rule 8.1" or describe any special procedure.

* 12.1 Individual recalls will be signalled ● .

Use only when a new warning signal is desired after a general recall.

12.2 When a general recall has been signalled, a new warning signal will be made one minute after the lowering of Code flag "First Substitute".

Use only for a multi-class regatta.

12.3 When a general recall has been signalled, the start(s) for the succeeding class(es) will be postponed accordingly.

13 Mark Boats

Insert the description of the flag or shape.

Mark boats will be stationed beyond each mark. At the finish, the mark boat will be stationed beyond the finishing line. When on station only, each mark boat will display a ● . Failure of a mark boat to be on station or to display her signal will not be grounds for redress.

14 Change of Course after the Start

14.1 When changing the course after the start, the race committee will lay a new mark and will lift the original mark as soon as practicable. Any mark to be rounded after rounding the new mark may be relocated to maintain the original course configuration.

Insert the sound signal.

14.2 A change of course will be signalled near the mark beginning the leg being changed by a race committee boat that will display Code flag "C" and the approximate compass bearing to the new mark and sound a ● periodically. The change will be signalled before the leading yacht has begun the leg, although the new mark may not yet be in position.

14.3 When in a subsequent change of course a new mark is replaced, it will be replaced with an original mark.

*15 The Finish

The finishing line will be between a staff displaying an orange flag or shape on a race committee boat and Mark 1 at the port end.

(OR)

The finishing line will be between a staff displaying an orange flag or shape on a race committee boat and the port end finishing mark.

(OR)

The finishing line will be between staffs displaying orange flags or shapes on two race committee boats.

*16 Time Limit

Insert the time(s) and class(es). Adjust for a single class regatta or for a single time limit for all classes.

The time limit will be ● for the ● class and ● for the ● class. Yachts finishing more than ● minutes after the first yacht finishes or after the time limit, whichever is later, will be scored "Did not finish".

17 Protests

Insert the location and time.

17.1 Protests shall be written on forms available at ● and lodged there within ● after the time of the last yacht's finish.

(OR)

Insert the location and time.

17.1 Protests shall be written on forms available at ● and lodged there within Protest Time which will begin ● and end ● later.

Substitute "race committee" or "protest committee" for "jury" when there is no jury. See above. Insert the time.

17.2 The jury will hear protests in approximately the order of receipt as soon as possible.

(OR)

17.2 The jury will hear protests in approximately the order of receipt beginning at ● .

177

17.3 Protest notices will be posted within 30 minutes of the protest time limit to inform competitors where and when there is a hearing in which they are parties to a protest or named as witnesses.

Use only when the requirements of rule 1.5 are met.

17.4 Decisions of the jury will be final in accordance with racing rule 1.5.

*18 Scoring

The Olympic Scoring System, Appendix 5.1 of the racing rules, will apply.

(OR)

Use when the Olympic Scoring System is desired but the number of scheduled races is other than seven. Insert the number of races. See Appendix 5.1 for other possible alterations.

The Olympic Scoring System, Appendix 5.1 of the racing rules, will apply, except that ● races are scheduled, of which ● races shall be completed to constitute a series.

See Appendix 5.2 for possible alterations.

(OR)

The Low-Point Scoring System, Appendix 5.2 of the racing rules, will apply.

(OR)

State the scoring system to apply by reference to the class rules or other document containing the complete scoring system.

_____

_____

_____

19 Alternative Penalties

The 720° Turns penalty, Appendix 3.1 of the racing rules, will apply.

(OR)

The Percentage penalty, Appendix 3.2 of the racing rules, will apply.

20 Support Boats

Insert the dates or times.

Team leaders, coaches and other support personnel shall not go afloat in the racing area between ● inclusive except in boats provided by the organising authority. The penalty for failing to comply with this requirement may be the disqualification of all yachts associated with the infringing support personnel.

21 Haul-out Restrictions

When this applies to some classes only, insert the name(s) of the class(es) between "all" and "yachts". Insert the time. Substitute "race committee" or "protest committee" for "jury" when there is no jury. Use (b) only when there is a scheduled reserve day.

All yachts shall be afloat before ● on the day preceding the first scheduled race and shall not be hauled out during the regatta except:

(a) with and according to the terms of prior written permission of the jury; or

(b) after the race preceding a reserve day. In which case they shall again be afloat before ● on the day preceding the next race.

22 Plastic Pools and Diving Equipment

Insert the class(es) and time.

Underwater breathing apparatus, plastic pools or their equivalent shall not be used around ● class yachts after ● on the day preceding the first scheduled race.

23 Radio Communication

A yacht shall neither make radio transmissions while racing nor receive special radio communications not available to all yachts.

24 Prizes

Alter as required. When perpetual trophies are to be awarded, refer to them by their complete names.

Prizes will be awarded to each member of the crews placing first, second and third in the regatta.

Appendix A—Illustrating the Course

Shown here is a recommended method for illustrating a course. Any course can be similarly shown, using the same details. When there is more than one course, prepare separate diagrams for each and state how each course will be signalled.

This course is a typical "Olympic" course: triangle, windward, leeward, windward, on a 45°-90°-45° triangle. In this example the starting and finishing lines are separate and are between two race committee boats. The third sentence of instruction 9.1 and the third versions of instructions 11.2 and 15 would be used.

Start-1-2-3-1-3-Finish
Marks to be rounded to port

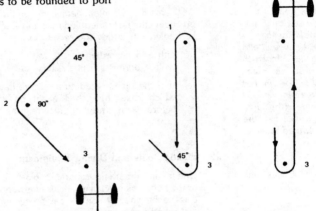

In the next example the course is the same except that the starting and finishing lines are between a race committee boat and Marks 3 and 1 respectively. The third sentence of instruction 9.1 would be deleted and the first versions of instructions 11.2 and 15 would be used.

Start-1-2-3-1-3-Finish
Marks to be rounded to port.

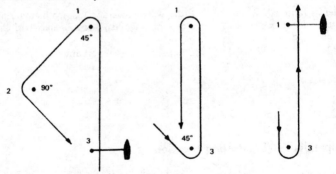

Appendix B—Yachts provided by the Organising Authority

The following sailing instruction should be used when all yachts will be provided by the organising authority.

The instruction can be added to or altered, or portions deleted to suit the situation. When used, it should be inserted following instruction 5, Signals Made Ashore.

X   Yachts

X.1   Yachts will be provided for all competitors, who shall not modify them or cause them to be modified in any way except that:

   (a) a compass may be tied or taped to the hull or spars;

   (b) wind indicators, including yarn or thread, may be tied or taped anywhere on the yacht;

   (c) hulls, centreboards and rudders may be cleaned only with water;

   (d) adhesive tape may be used anywhere above the water line; and

   (e) all fittings or equipment designed to be adjusted may be adjusted, provided that the class rules are observed.

X.2   All equipment provided with the yacht for sailing purposes shall be carried while afloat.

X.3   The penalty for infringement of the above instructions will be disqualification from all races sailed in contravention of the instruction.

Substitute "race committee" or "protest committee" for "jury" when there is no jury.

X.4   Competitors shall report any damage or loss of equipment, however slight, to the organising authority's representative immediately after securing the yacht ashore. The penalty for infringement of this instruction, unless the jury is satisfied that the competitor made a determined effort to comply, will be disqualification from the race most recently sailed.

Use when the regatta is not restricted to class members.

X.5   Class rules requiring competitors to be members of the class association will not apply.

Appendix C—Gate Start

When this instruction is used, instruction 9, The Course, should show the starting area on the diagram, indicating the Port Limit Mark. This instruction replaces instruction 11, The Start. Instruction 12.1 will not be used.

11 Gate Start

11.1 Starting marks will be:

Describe the mark.

    (a) The Port Limit Mark, a ● on the starboard side of the race committee boat.

    (b) The Pathfinder.

    (c) The Gate Launch, displaying Code flag "G".

    (d) The Guard Boat, displaying Code flag "U".

Insert the system to be used. Insert the number of minutes.

11.2 The signals for starting will be in accordance with racing rule 4.4(a) System ● displayed from the race committee boat, which will also display Code flag "G", signifying a gate start. At or before the warning signal, numeral pendant ● will be displayed indicating the time in minutes between the starting signal and the time at which the Gate Launch will stop at the starboard end of the starting line.

11.3 The Pathfinder for the first race sailed will be appointed by the race committee. The Pathfinder for subsequent races will be the yacht that finished tenth in the preceding race. When this yacht is unable to race or has acted as Pathfinder previously, the Pathfinder will be appointed by the race committee and will normally be the yacht that finished eleventh in the preceding race. The national letters and sail number of the Pathfinder will be posted on the official notice board each day. Prior to the preparatory signal, the Pathfinder shall report to the Gate Launch, which will be near the Port Limit Mark.

11.4 After the preparatory signal, yachts shall not sail on the windward side of an imaginary line which would be the course of a yacht sailing from the Port Limit Mark on a close-hauled port tack.

11.5 Approximately ten seconds prior to the starting signal:

    (a) the Pathfinder will begin a close-hauled port tack from the Port Limit Mark,

(b) the Gate Launch will keep station close astern of the Pathfinder, and

(c) the Guard Boat may escort the Pathfinder on her starboard side.

11.6 The starting line (except for the Pathfinder) will be between the Port Limit Mark and the centre of the stern of the Gate Launch.

11.7 All yachts (except for the Pathfinder) shall start on starboard tack after the starting signal. A yacht starting prematurely shall retire from the race. Racing rule 8.1, Individual Recall, shall not apply.

11.8 The Pathfinder shall sail her close-hauled course until she is released by hail from the Gate Launch, after which she may continue on port tack or tack, as she wishes.

11.9 After the release of the Pathfinder, the Gate Launch will continue her course and speed until the gate has been opened for the period signalled in instruction 11.2. She will then stop, make a long sound signal, drift for one minute, and finally signal the close of the gate by lowering Code flag "G" with a short sound signal. Thereafter, no yacht shall start.

11.10 Before *starting*, a yacht shall not interfere with the Pathfinder. Any yacht that interferes with, or passes between, or attempts to pass between the Pathfinder, the Gate Launch or the Guard Boat, or that causes another yacht to interfere in any of these ways, or that is on the port side of the Gate Launch as she opens the gate, shall retire from that race and shall be ineligible for any re-starts of that race, unless the infringing yacht can satisfy the race committee that her actions were caused either by another yacht not having right of way, or by some other unavoidable circumstance. Racing rule 8.2(b) shall not apply.

APPENDIX 14—Event Classification and Advertising

(No changes are contemplated before 1993. However, the Permanent Committee may approve changes in the interim.)

1   General

1.1   This appendix shall apply when *racing* and, in addition, unless otherwise prescribed in the notice of race, from 0700 on the first race day of a regatta or series until the expiry of the time limit for lodging protests following the last race of the regatta or series.

1.2   Events shall be classified as Category A, B or C in accordance with paragraphs 2, 3 and 4 of this appendix. Unless otherwise prescribed in the notice of race and the sailing instructions, an event shall be classified as Category A.

1.3   The notice of race and the sailing instructions for any category of event may prescribe more restrictive criteria than are otherwise required for that category.

1.4   The IYRU, a national authority, the Offshore Racing Council (ORC) or a class association may develop rules for sanctioning events within its jurisdiction in any or all categories, as well as for giving consent for individual advertisements. Fees may be required.

1.5   Advertised products shall comply with moral and ethical standards.

1.6   In world and continental events, unless so prescribed by the class rules, a competitor shall not be required or induced to display advertising on a yacht, clothing or equipment.

1.7   Governmental requirements affecting yachts shall override this appendix only to the extent that they are inconsistent with it.

1.8   The following advertising is permitted at all times:

   (a)   one sailmaker's mark (which may include the name or mark of the manufacturer of the sail cloth and pattern or model description of the sail) may be displayed on each side of any sail. The whole of such a mark shall be placed not more than 15% of the length of the foot of the sail or 300 mm from its tack, whichever is the greater. This latter limitation shall not apply to the position of marks on spinnakers.

   (b)   one builder's mark (which may include the name or mark of the designer) may be placed on the hull, and one maker's mark may be displayed on spars and equipment.

   (c)   such marks (or plates) shall fit within a square not exceeding 150 mm × 150 mm.

(d) one maker's mark may be displayed on each item of clothing and equipment worn by the crew, provided that the mark fits within a square not exceeding 100 mm × 100 mm.

(e) the yacht's type may be displayed once on each side of the hull, provided that the lettering shall not exceed 1% in height and 5% in length of the overall length of the yacht, but not exceeding a maximum height of 100 mm and a maximum length of 700 mm.

(f) a sailboard's type may be displayed on the hull in two places. The lettering shall not exceed 200 mm in height.

1.9 After obtaining the approval, when relevant, of the national authority, ORC and/or class association, the organising authority of a sponsored event may permit or require advertising by the sponsor on yachts and sailboards only within the following limitations:

(a) On yachts: the display of a flag and/or the application to the hulls of a decal or sticker, neither of which shall be larger than 45 cm × 60 cm.

(b) On sailboards: the display of not more than two stickers, one on each side of the sail, each of which shall fit within a rectangle of 2,500 cm², none of the sides of which shall exceed 80 cm in length. The notice of race shall state whether one or both sides of the sail are to be used. When both sides are used, the stickers shall be placed back to back. The stickers shall be placed above the wishbone and at least partly in the lower half of the sail.

(c) Such permission or requirement shall be prescribed in the notice of race.

1.10 When a **protest committee** after finding the facts decides that a yacht or her crew has infringed this appendix, rule 74.4, Penalties and Exoneration, shall not apply, and the **protest committee** shall:

(a) warn the infringing yacht that a further infringement will result in action under rule 70.2, Action by Race or Protest Committee, or

(b) disqualify the yacht, or

(c) when the infringement occurs when the yacht is not *racing,* disqualify the yacht from the race most recently *sailed* or from the next race *sailed* after the infringement, or

(d) when it decides that there was a gross breach of the appendix, disqualify the yacht from more than one race or from the whole series.

2   Category A

Except as permitted in accordance with paragraphs 1.8 and 1.9, a yacht competing in a Category A event shall not display advertising on her hull, spars, sails and equipment and, while aboard the yacht, on the clothing and equipment worn by the crew.

3   Category B

In addition to the advertising permitted by paragraphs 1.8 and 1.9, a yacht competing in a Category B event may display advertising only in accordance with paragraphs 3.1 to 3.4, and a sailboard in accordance with paragraph 3.5.

3.1   ADVERTISING ON YACHTS—GENERAL

(a)   A yacht shall not display the advertisements of more than two organisations at one time.

(b)   Each advertisement shall consist of one or two of the following:

(i)   the name of the organisation;

(ii)   one brand or product name;

(iii)   one logo.

3.2   ADVERTISING ON HULLS

(a)   The forward 25% of the length overall of the hull, including the deck, shall be clear of any individual advertising. This area is reserved for the requirements of the IYRU, national authorities, the ORC or class associations.

(b)   50% of the remaining 75% of the length overall of the hull may be used for individual advertising.

3.3   ADVERTISING ON SAILS

(a)   Advertising on spinnakers is without restriction, except as provided in paragraph 3.3(c).

(b)   On other sails, only one advertisement may be carried at any one time, and it may be on both sides of one sail. It shall be placed below an imaginary line between the mid-points of the luff and leech of the sail, and have a width of not more than two-thirds of the length of the foot of the sail and a height of not more than one-third of that width.

(c)   Advertisements on all sails shall be clearly separated from, and below, the sail numbers.

3.4   ADVERTISING ON SPARS

(a)   One-third of the main mast may be used.

(b)   Two-thirds of the main boom may be used.

(c)   Advertising on the mast or boom shall be limited to the name, or logo of one of the organisations.

3.5 ADVERTISING ON SAILBOARDS

(a) The upper half of the sail above the wishbone may carry only the logo of a sailboard manufacturer.

(b) The tack corner on each side of the sail may carry one label or logo either of a sailboard manufacturer or a sailmaker.

(c) The lower half of the sail above the wishbone may carry only the logo of a sailmaker.

(d) The space below the wishbone is at the disposal of the competitor for advertising. Any advertising shall fit within a rectangle of 4000 cm².

3.6 ADVERTISING ON CLOTHING AND PERSONAL EQUIPMENT
In addition to the advertisements carried on the yacht or sailboard, advertisements limited to the organisation(s) advertising on the yacht or sailboard and one or two additional organisations may be displayed on clothing and equipment worn by the crew.

4 Category C

In addition to the advertising permitted by paragraphs 1.8 and 1.9, a yacht competing in a Category C event may display advertising in accordance with special advertising rules. Such rules shall be:

(a) prescribed or approved by the national authority for an event within its jurisdiction;

(b) subject to approval by the IYRU; and

(c) stated in the notice of race and the sailing instructions.